# Dyslexia in the Early Years

## A practical guide to teaching and learning

## Dimitra Hartas

Routledge
Taylor & Francis Group

LONDON AND NEW YORK

This book is dedicated to Pavlos and Victor, who remind me constantly of the beauty and inquisitiveness of young children's mind, and their immense capacity for relating and bonding emotionally with others.

First published 2006
by Routledge
2 Park Square, Milton Park, Abingdon, Oxon OX14 4RN

Simultaneously published in the USA and Canada
by Routledge
270 Madison Ave, New York, NY 10016

*Routledge is an imprint of the Taylor & Francis Group*

© 2006 Dimitra Hartas

Typeset in Times New Roman and Gill Sans by
Integra Software Services Pvt. Ltd, Pondicherry, India
Printed and bound in Great Britain by
Bell & Bain Ltd, Glasgow

*British Library Cataloguing-in-Publication Data*
A catalogue record for this book is available from the British Library

*Library of Congress Cataloging-in-Publication Data*
Hartas, Dimitra, 1966–
    Dyslexia in the early years : a practical guide to teaching and
    learning / Dimitra Hartas.
        p.   cm.
    Includes bibliographical references and index.
    ISBN 0–415–34500–6 (pbk : alk. paper)
    1. Dyslexic children—Education (Early childhood)
    2. Learning disabled children—Education (Early childhood)
    3. Dyslexia.   I. Title.
    LC4708.H37 2006
    371.91′44—dc22

                                2005012693

ISBN10: 0–415–34500–6
ISBN13: 9–78–0–415–34500–2

# Contents

# Preface

With early years education becoming increasingly prescriptive, widely debated issues in education such as accountability, raising the standards in literacy and numeracy, the introduction of the national curriculum, inspection systems, professional development and the 'new professionalism' also extend to early years settings. Moreover, new challenging perspectives of children's development and learning, the influence of the home environment, the diversity in child rearing practices, and the quality of the interactions between children and parents/teachers become particularly relevant in the context of early years education. Finally, the debate on difference and diversity, and the contentious nature and 'invisibility' of dyslexia and other areas of 'need' continue to shape early years teaching and learning.

These new conceptualisations of childhood, the conflicting notions of diversity and the changing understandings of young children's educational and everyday experiences are likely to shape early years education in ways that are not yet fully understood. Children occupy what Rosaldo (1993) describes as 'cultural borderlands' in that their experiences may be located in more than one culture. Along these lines, children may also occupy linguistic, ethnic and social 'borderlands', functioning within different and, at times, conflicting worlds. This is particularly true for children who present multiple facets of diversity, such as EAL (English as an Additional Language) children, children with restricted emotional experiences and stressful upbringing, and children living on the margins of the dominant culture.

In this climate, early years practitioners face many challenges. A major challenge is to engage in responsive and responsible pedagogy by treating young children as citizens with rights equal to those of adults and broadening their understanding of the world while operating within constraints, e.g. curriculum, low status of early years work, limited training. An equally challenging endeavour is to embrace diversity and difference and support children to reach their potential.

Research on the effectiveness of early years education has come into a full circle by providing evidence that good quality of early years learning is directly linked to the quality of the relationships and emotional bonds formed between early years staff and children. It is refreshing to see that, in education, the significance of emotional attachment for children's learning and social development is re-visited, acknowledging that education and care should not be separated. It is also hopeful that early years education has the potential to counterbalance the effects of social disadvantage through social change.

My goal for writing this book is to provide research-based guidance on classroom practice by taking into account current policy, and link theoretical and practical implications. Although it is tempting to take a recipe-style approach to teaching and learning, especially given the urgency of supporting early years practitioners, it is important to balance everyday classroom practice with theory by discussing research that is relevant to early years practitioners' work.

# Foreword

Through the 1970s and 1980s, from before the time of the *Warnock Report* (1978), there has been considerable debate about terms such as 'dyslexia' and 'specific learning difficulty'. This took place in a climate of integration practices where the focus on assessment was shifting away from identification that may have placed too much emphasis on 'within-child' determinants of learning and too little attention to the conditions of instruction. Meanwhile, the 1990s have seen the introduction of a national curriculum and assessment and a system of school inspection in order to monitor the overall quality of inclusive schooling on a regular basis. Indeed, the gathering concern about educational standards, in national and international terms, has led to the introduction of a National Literacy Strategy (NLS) (DfEE, 1998) as part of which all primary schools have available to them a specially devised framework for teaching word, sentence and text level work. Whilst in the context of special education, the introduction of a revised Code of Practice in 2001 has brought a staged process of assessment through teaching.

In 1998, the Division of Educational and Child Psychology (DECP) of The British Psychological Society convened a working party chaired by Rea Reason to write a report making recommendations about the concept of dyslexia and the principles of assessment related to it. The focus of this was on younger school-age children. The following definition was adopted:

> *This focuses on literacy learning at the 'word level' and implies that the problem is severe and persistent despite appropriate learning opportunities. It provides the basis of a staged process of assessment through teaching.*

The report also examined alternative theoretical accounts of dyslexia and took account of instructional, interpersonal and emotional factors in the individual child. Central to English educational psychology practice is the understanding of reciprocal effects of cognitive processes, instructional conditions and the young learner's perceptions and experiences.

According to the report, phonological coding provided a central unifying thread in the word reading process. Phonology was seen in terms of processing sounds in words rather than their meanings or grammatical structures though the role, amount and relative weight of phonological processes and how complete these might need to be was not yet clear and, in any case, might alter in the course of reading development. Indeed, De Lemos (2002: 5), in a recent systematic review of evidence for the Australian Centre for Educational Research, has concluded that phonological awareness has been found to have the strongest causal relationship to word reading skill and is also the most amenable to instruction. This is why it is usually noted in the literature as being critical to the acquisition of literacy.

This leaves a number of unresolved questions that relate to young children in the early stages of literacy acquisition:

- How long should one wait before concluding that 'accurate and fluent' word reading and/or spelling is developing 'very incompletely' and 'with great difficulty'?
- How can one quantify 'severe and persistent'?
- How does one determine cut-off points between mild and possibly temporary difficulties and those severe and more long-standing dyslexic difficulties that entitle the young child to special provision?

These questions cannot be addressed without consideration of the age and developmental status of the learner or the nature and degree of instructional effort already expended. In other words, environmental influences and learning opportunities are a central consideration. Assessment from this perspective will be carried out in the context of what is known about the child's language and literacy developmental history in general and, specifically, the methods of learning and teaching received. In England, for example, this means the framework and structured word, sentence and text level content of the NLS for children of five onwards which is structured to include word, sentence and text level work for each age group and includes the final year of the new Foundation Stage curriculum (DfEE, 2000) for three- to five-year-old children. Problems have already been identified, however, with targets set for Year 1 (children aged five to six years) where the pace for pupils with learning and/or dyslexic-type difficulties may be too fast and coverage too superficial. Whilst it is beyond the scope of this short foreword to consider the NLS content, central to identification and intervention must be the belief that support for dyslexia is not something different from what is available in the inclusive, mainstream classroom, that is, it will need to be appropriate for a wide range of learners with different achievements, aptitudes and strategies. The British Dyslexia Association, for instance, has recently emphasised the importance of 'dyslexia friendly schools'.

With the increased knowledge, awareness and attention placed on literacy learning, monitoring intervention can take place early enough to ensure that learners with persistent difficulties do not experience a delay in receiving targeted support. Encouraging teachers and carers to 'notice' and be aware of children's individual needs as well as 'adjust' their responses accordingly is in line with assessment, intervention and monitoring in the Code of Practice and provides a common terminology for formative assessment from the new Foundation Stage Profile for five-year-olds and a baseline for observations, curriculum-based assessment and future teaching plans.

In writing this book, Dimitra Hartas has taken full account of the current policy to practice context and yet adopted a realistic and holistic approach to young children's learning that emphasises the importance of partnerships with parents and professionals. In so doing, she is able to examine sensitively the effectiveness of classroom strategies and methods of teaching literacy for young children with dyslexia, as well as the use of Information and Communication Technology (ICT) to support staff training and children's learning. Overall, she has created a comprehensive yet very accessible text that links theoretical and practical considerations, as well as generating plans of action to promote literacy learning and curriculum access to young dyslexic learners in a context of inclusionary practices.

Carol Aubrey

## Acknowledgement

I wish to acknowledge Professor Carol Aubrey who kindly gave her time to read through the manuscript, for providing constructive feedback and writing the foreword to this book.

Dimitra Hartas<br>University of Warwick

# Introduction

## An overview of early years education

At the beginning of the 21st century, many developed and developing countries have shown an urgency to re-define and re-think early years education and care as a profession. Recent developments in early childhood policy and practice in the Scandinavian countries (i.e. Sweden, Finland, Norway) provide challenging perspectives about child rearing practices, early years education and notions of childhood. Childhood is not experienced in a vacuum in that children's emotional, social, intellectual and physical development is intimately connected to and dependent upon the social-cultural and political reality of the society in which they live. The quality of the interaction between children and their educators, as well as the strength of the emotional bonds they build with their caregivers, influences their development within the wider social context (Gammage, 2003).

New understandings about childhood have implications for the provision of education and care and the roles and responsibilities of early years practitioners, fuelling on-going debates about children's needs and rights. Increasingly, young children are perceived as being capable of co-constructing learning during social interactions with minimum adult assistance and scaffolding, challenging dominant Vygotskian ideas regarding the zone of proximal development. In this context, early years professionals are expected to respond to the shifts in our perceptions of childhood by moving away from the provision of fragmented services through diagnosing and monitoring children's 'needs' and the skills that they 'do not have', to embrace pedagogy and ascertain children's rights.

Our views of childhood have also implications for defending children's rights. As Aubrey and her colleagues argue 'our images of children are social constructions which, whenever we are aware of it or not, serve particular purposes' (2000: 22). Furthermore, notions of citizenship are widened to apply to young children who, according to Moss and Petrie, are 'young citizens with rights equal to those of adults' (2002: 40). However, there are moral dilemmas to be resolved when considering young children's views and feelings regarding their education in that, because of their young age, they may not be able to articulate their concerns resulting in adults 'talking for them'.

## The importance of early years education

The early years of children's life are ones of rapid growth and development. Among educators and parents, there is a growing acceptance that good quality early years education and care broaden children's learning and social and emotional experiences by giving them a sense of belonging and supporting them to become confident and secure, eager and enthusiastic learners.

Moreover, good quality of early years education is central to children's learning and development of social skills, such as negotiation and conflict resolution skills, ability to take others' perspective and show empathy and language and communication skills for accessing the curriculum and engaging in peer interactions. Current notions of literacy are constantly expanding to include social and emotional literacy, resilience, resourcefulness and adaptability to change. Thus, catering for young children with dyslexia requires early years practitioners to take a holistic approach towards their learning by considering their language and social-emotional development and the dynamics of the interactions with their caregivers, families and communities.

The quality of early years education has been the subject of ongoing debates, interest and radical re-shaping nationally and internationally. Around the world, UNICEF and UNESCO have invested human and financial capital to promote education and care for young children. Up until recently, in the UK, legislation, policy and practice for early years education have been less prescriptive, mostly relying on local initiatives and neighbourhood schemes. Lately, however, early years education has become an important item in the British political agenda with the new Labour government showing commitment to reducing poverty and combating social exclusion through the provision of early years education.

Numerous national governmental and non-governmental initiatives have raised the status of early years education by stimulating major changes in the public's attitudes and understandings of the educational needs of young children, the role of professionals and the legislation that underlies early years policy and practice (Aubrey, 2004). Moreover, governmental initiatives, such as Sure Start, aim at introducing social reforms by providing good quality of education and care for young children and opportunities for their parents and caregivers to return to work.

## Early years policy and practice

In the UK, the revised SEN Code of Practice (DfES, 2001), governmental initiatives (e.g. Sure Start) and non-governmental organisations (e.g. British Dyslexia Association) have all stressed the importance of supporting young children's learning and social-emotional adjustment. Also, the development of a whole-school Special Educational Needs (SEN) policy and practice for Nursery and Reception settings have become more pressing than ever. Lloyd argues that if early years education is thought to be beneficial for children in general, it is 'doubly crucial' for young children with SEN (2002).

The SEN Code of Practice placed early years education in a legal context, establishing a three-stage intervention to identify and support young children's diverse needs. There is an increasing expectation that early years practitioners will respond to LEA's legal requirements to meet the diverse needs of young children within the framework of the National Curriculum, work closely with parents and other professionals and, last but not least, develop a broad vision with respect to the principles, rights and entitlement of young children with SEN. The emphasis on SEN provision in terms of identifying, assessing, planning and teaching children with diverse needs has increased early years staff's anxiety, who feel that they are not adequately prepared to face these multiple challenges.

Moreover, the Code of Practice stresses the rights and responsibilities as introduced by the Disability Act 2001 and the United Nations Convention on the Rights of the Child by emphasising pupil participation and parental involvement in every aspect of the decision-making regarding educational provision. Involving parents and ascertaining children's views have particular implications for early years education given that learning initiatives and classroom practice for this age group are influenced greatly by children's family practices and orientation.

Another major change in early years provision is the implementation of inspection systems. Ofsted inspections will be now carried out across the full range of early years provision to ensure effectiveness in their inclusive policies and practices. Specifically, the inspectors will look at how well early years settings reach out to all learners, and the practical steps they take to consider young children's varied life, experiences and social-cultural and ethnic backgrounds. With the increasing pressure of ofsted inspection, early years teachers and other practitioners are expected to achieve measurable learning outcomes with the danger that social activities, such as play, will either be neglected or become 'curricularised' (Strandell, 2000: 148).

## Early years curriculum

Over the last decade of the 20th century, major changes have taken place in early years curriculum, moving from the Desirable Outcomes for Children's Learning in 1996 to the revised Early Years Goals in 1999 and, finally, to the Curriculum Guidance for the Foundation Stage in 2000. These changes have been stimulated by the recognition that the early years curriculum should be well articulated and relevant to young children's educational and social needs. Curricular changes are part of an overall shift in early years policy and practice regarding young children's learning, leaving early years practitioners hanging somewhere in between. Although the Desirable Outcomes for Children's Learning (SCAA, 1996) did not intend to 'tell practitioners what to do' (Carr and May, 2000: 62), a large number of early years staff do not have the necessary training and experience to translate policy into practice effectively (e.g. Browne, 1998).

The Curriculum Guidance for the Foundation Stage (QCA, 2000) acknowledges that children learn in different ways and encounter new learning experiences constantly. It also acknowledges the important role that early years practitioners play. Specifically, it states:

> Children, aged three, four and five are constantly encountering new experiences and seeking to understand them in order to extent their skills, develop their confidence and build on what they already know. They learn in many different ways. Practitioners have a crucial role in this learning and should draw on a range of teaching and care strategies and knowledge of child development.
>
> (QCA/DfEE, 2000: 6)

This framework refers to learning experiences based on different key aspects of children's development and learning. The early years curriculum framework aims at supporting staff to plan activities and experiences that promote children's development and learning in:

- personal, social and emotional development
- communication, language and literacy

- mathematical concept
- knowledge and understanding of the world
- expressive and aesthetic/creative development
- physical development and movement (QCA, 2000).

In this book, some of these areas of development, namely language/communication and social-emotional development will be explored with regard to young children with dyslexia, and practical guidance will be provided to inform classroom practice. Almost all chapters in this book are organised around language/communication, literacy and social-emotional development in children with dyslexia, raising issues of effective teaching and learning to support young children's acquisition of literacy skills, knowledge and understanding of the world.

It is widely recognised that young children's learning is influenced, to a great extent, by their own experiences gained during the social interactions with their caregivers and educators, highlighting the crucial role that early years practitioners play in shaping children's education (Sammons, Elliot, Sylva, Melhuish, Siraj-Blatchford, Taggart, 2004). With this understanding in mind, early years practitioners are expected to undertake multiple roles, be aware of the social-cultural dynamics of children's family and community contexts, work with parents and other professionals/agencies and support children's social interactions with peers and adults.

## The early years practitioner's role: rewards and challenges

Recently, the nature of the work of early years practitioners (e.g. nursery nurses, reception staff) is undergoing a major transformation. The introduction of early years curriculum, inspection systems, the new national standards for qualified teacher status and legislative frameworks (e.g. SEN Code of Practice) have changed the landscape of early years provision. Moreover, the 'new professionalism', as McCulloch *et al.* (2000) argue, sets high expectations for staff working in early years settings. In this climate, preparing early years educators to face and respond to these challenges is not an easy undertaking.

The role of early years practitioners is multifaceted with many paradoxical aspects. Because of the nature of their work in early years settings and the age of the children involved, it is difficult to separate the role of parent/caregiver and that of formal teacher/staff. On one hand, a separation of roles is thought to support accountability, raise performance standards and maintain a professional image (Moyles, 2001). On the other hand, combining these seemingly conflicting roles can be particularly important to meet the emotional and learning needs of young children.

Early years practitioners are required to form effective links with parents and other professionals and agencies through the development of successful partnerships by understanding, valuing and building on children's learning and social-emotional experiences before and during their pre-school years. Research into pre-school teaching has shown that early years educators find the experience of working closely with young children's families and communities worthwhile and rewarding (Pollard and Filer, 1999). This is an interesting finding especially at a time where the value placed on young children's education is low as reflected in low salaries and job status and limited opportunities for training and qualifications for early years practitioners (Moyles, 2001).

Early years practitioners are increasingly expected to deal with multiple facets of diversity in pupils' profiles and needs, including SEN. Wolfendale argues that 'many practitioners who have solid early years experience base do not have commensurate SEN experience' (2000: 147). Yet, reception teachers and other early years practitioners are required to carry out SEN and inclusion initiatives, collaborate with parents and professionals, assess, plan and apply classroom differentiation techniques to support young children with diverse learning and developmental needs. Moreover, the new National Standards for Qualified Teacher Status (September, 2002) has identified new priorities, namely teaching English as an Additional Language (EAL) and placed a considerable emphasis on professional values, accentuating the challenges that early years staff already face. Thus, bridging the existing gap between early years education and practitioners' knowledge about SEN and EAL policy and practice has become more pressing than ever.

## A family-centred early years education

The current conceptualisations of early years education as a vehicle for social reform at a family and community level is empowering. The Organisation for Economic Co-operation and Development recognises that good quality of early years education has a dual function, namely setting the stage for children's academic achievement and life-long learning, and supporting the social needs of their families (OECD, 2001a). Indeed, a unique feature of early years education is its focus on both individual children and their family/community, where young children's experiences are located and intertwined with social and cultural practices.

Taking into consideration children's experiences and interactions with their parents/caregivers is crucial. The findings from the EPPE study suggest that it is not 'who the parents are but what they do' with their children that matters. These findings should make us re-think Bourdieu's conceptualisation of social-cultural capital and its links to academic achievement (1973). The notion of social-cultural capital should be widened in that, for young children, social-emotional capital is evidenced through their close relationships with extended family and friends, family traditions and the emotional bonds they form with their parents and caregivers, regardless of their family's socio-economic status. Thus, restricted notions of cultural/social capital as an advantage acquired through middle-class practices, values, social networks and economic affluence ought to be challenged when looking closely at the dynamics of child/caregiver interactions.

Moreover, generic notions of deficits in the community and lack of social-cultural capital associated with children from low socio-economic background are less helpful, especially as children are increasingly capable of co-constructing their learning and social experiences. Undoubtedly, children's school and life experiences can be adversely affected by poverty and social deprivation; however, it is an over-simplification to think that young children from environments considered to be economically and socially deprived are necessarily lacking in rich learning, linguistic and social experiences. Socio-economic deprivation should not be equated with emotional deprivation and reduced learning experiences, or what Jacques called 'the loss of intimacy' between parents and children. The strength of the emotional bonds and interactions between children and their parents have the potential to counterbalance difficult circumstances triggered by poverty and social exclusion from the dominant culture.

## Classroom guidance

The guidance regarding classroom practice offered in this book is organised along four inter-related strands, namely pre-literacy strategies, language/communication strategies, literacy strategies (e.g. reading, spelling and writing) and social-emotional strategies (e.g. self-esteem building, social skills development, friendship development). Grouping classroom support along these aspects of children's development is based on evidence suggesting that children with dyslexia are likely to display learning and social-emotional difficulties, as well as difficulties with the acquisition of language (e.g. speech, listening, comprehension) and pre-literacy skills (e.g. phonological awareness, orientation, sequencing, short-term memory).

In this book, pre-literacy, literacy, language and social-emotional classroom strategies will be presented within the framework of differentiation in a variety of classroom structures (e.g. circle time, peer-mediated learning). The National Curriculum has provided teachers and other classroom staff with a model to assist them to carry out differentiation successfully by focusing on learning objectives, teaching styles and access to learning (NLS, 2000). Learning objectives refer to the outcomes decided for pupils with SEN that are different from those set for the rest of the class, ensuring that the objectives match the individual children's strengths and respond to their needs. Teaching styles refer to a variety of methods regarding the planning and delivery of the curriculum. Modifying teaching styles by, for example, adopting a multi-sensory approach in terms of using different ways to present information such as visual, verbal or kinaesthetic lies in the heart of differentiation. Finally, access to learning involves removing obstacles although the learning objectives remain the same for all children, with some additional systems in place to support children with SEN. For example, communication aid devices for children with hearing impairment are likely to remove obstacles towards learning by facilitating the development of listening and speaking skills, enabling children understand instructions and participate actively in classroom discussions (Gross, 2002).

## About this book

This book is intended for early years practitioners mainly. Its aim is to introduce pre-school and reception teachers as well as other early years staff (e.g. nursery nurses, learning support assistants) to the knowledge and practical understanding required to develop the confidence to handle their increasing professional demands and respond to the diverse needs of young children with dyslexia.

The present book is organised along seven chapters. Chapter 1 introduces readers to dyslexia, discusses its controversial nature and presents characteristics and early indicators of dyslexia to raise awareness among early years practitioners. Chapter 2 focuses on language development and language difficulties in the context of early years, and explores the possibility of a co-existence between language/communication difficulties and dyslexia in young children. Chapter 3 takes an integrated approach by placing dyslexia in the context of social-emotional difficulties and language/communication concerns. Understanding the relationship between language and social-emotional difficulties and their impact on literacy has important practical implications for differentiated teaching. Chapter 4 explores issues of assessment and identification of literacy, language and social-emotional difficulties in young children. It raises concerns regarding the process of diagnosing young children, and argues for the need to take what Lindsay describes as a 'systemic approach' towards identifying children's strengths and needs and informing teaching and classroom practice (2004). Chapter 5 addresses issues of effectiveness in early years teaching and learning by focusing on the curriculum and the National Literacy Strategy, and explores the roles and responsibilities of early years practitioners.

Chapter 6 discusses the use of ICT for the dual purpose of facilitating learning in young children with dyslexia and supporting early years staff's training needs and work practices. Chapter 6 also suggests strategies in which computers and IT can help young children with dyslexia, providing many practical examples. Finally, Chapter 7 focuses on early years practitioners' collaborative workings with parents, other adults in the classroom and outside agencies, raising issues of parental involvement, rights and inter-professional collaboration.

In writing this book, my goals are to:

- consider policy and practice in early years education by discussing current legislative frameworks (e.g. NLS, SEN Code of Practice, early years curriculum);
- approach young children's learning and social experiences not as distinct skills but holistically, by looking at the interplay between areas of development, namely social-emotional development, language and literacy;
- emphasise the importance of partnerships between parents, early years staff (e.g. nursery/reception teachers, learning support assistants) and outside agencies;
- reflect on the changing face of today's families and the ways in which parents are involved in their children's education;
- discuss the effectiveness of teaching methods/classroom strategies suggested to support literacy, language and social-emotional development in young children with dyslexia;
- reflect on the implications of the new professionalism for early years staff by discussing their roles and responsibilities and the challenges they face; and
- discuss the appropriateness of ICT in early years and ways in which early years staff use ICT to support their training needs and children's learning.

The teaching methods and classroom strategies to support young children with dyslexia offered in this book should not be taken as subscriptions but as research-based suggestions that have been found to be effective with some children. There is no guarantee that the recommended strategies will be effective for all children with dyslexia across early years settings. However, it is important to adopt a systematic and evidence-based approach in planning and implementing teaching and learning strategies for young children with dyslexia. It is equally crucial to keep an open mind with regard to the theories and social/political perspectives that underlie educational practice, rather than subscribe to one theoretical position or be influenced by populist attitudes and ideology towards early years education.

This book has been written with the understanding of the considerable pressure on your time, as a practitioner. Thus, the suggested classroom strategies involve individual work with children in a setting where the teacher receives support from other early years staff (e.g. learning support assistants), and whole-class activities that encourage children working together, allowing you and other classroom staff to focus on other aspects of your work.

I hope you find this book interesting and thought provoking, capable of assisting you with the everyday reality and challenges of meeting the learning, language and social-emotional needs of children with dyslexia. Apart from the suggestions offered for classroom practice, I hope that this book will stimulate the reflective practitioner in you and set the scene for ongoing discussions and debates on the experience of childhood and the quality of early years education and care, especially for SEN children.

# Chapter 1

# Dyslexia in young learners

## Introduction

The purpose of this chapter is to introduce readers to dyslexia, discuss its controversial nature and raise awareness among early years staff with regard to early characteristics and pointers of dyslexia and their impact on the development of pre-literacy skills. I would like to start this chapter by reflecting on young children as learners and on the process of learning. I will then introduce the term of Special Educational Needs (SEN) by elaborating on areas of need typically displayed by young children with dyslexia, and discuss the conceptual differences between SEN and special needs. Finally, this chapter will conclude with classroom strategies to support the development of pre-literacy or emergent literacy skills in children with dyslexia.

## Young children as learners

Young children are active and experienced learners with natural curiosity, resilience and a lot of enthusiasm. They are unique individuals eager to make sense of their world, form emotional bonds and relationships with others, develop the capacity for empathy, learn and expand their horizons. Children acquire knowledge of the world in many different ways; however, they learn best in environments where they feel safe, secure and confident with many opportunities for play and enjoyment (Browne, 1998).

The developmental and learning needs of young children are different in nature from those of primary school children. Young children's experiences of the world are formed within the family mainly and thus, from an educational point of view, it is important to recognise their family's social-cultural practices and patterns of interaction. Pre-school children need encouragement from adults to explore their interests, develop a sustained concentration and engage in learning tasks and activities. Although children are capable of constructing their own understanding of the world, adults naturally scaffold their learning by providing daily opportunities to practise newly developed skills, gain educational and social-emotional experiences and become confident in their interactions with others. Parents and early years practitioners facilitate learning and social-emotional development in children by listening to what they say, having realistic expectations of them and planning and organising activities flexibly by considering children's interests and developmental needs.

Our understanding of how children learn changes continuously. Much of the theory and practice in education have been influenced by the 'literacy readiness' model which states that children need to be taught pre-requisite skills before they enter formal education (Miller, 2000). In contrast, the 'emergent literacy' model has given a very different view of children's learning by emphasising young children's attitudes and behaviour with regard to learning rather than how much they should know before they enter 'conventional literacy' (Sulzby, 1990: p. 85).

The main assumption of the emergent literacy model is that young children are active learners and not empty vessels that need to be taught specific skills to function in a formal education setting. This model also suggests that the acquisition of pre-literacy skills should not be constrained within the school and curricular frameworks but manifested in children's everyday interactions with caregivers and peers, play and explorations of their environment. The emergent literacy model values incidental learning where children learn by being exposed to everyday experiences without the need of direct and focused teaching. Incidental learning normally takes place through play which sets the platform for language, social skills and symbolic skills to be learned and consolidated, and for relationships to be formed and new ideas to be explored and expressed. Moreover, through play and everyday experiences, children learn how to collaborate with others, become confident in expressing their ideas and feelings, take initiatives and enjoy imagination games by engaging in 'pretend' situations (Riley, 2003).

Both the literacy readiness and the emergent literacy models of children's learning have influenced the way we support children who do not acquire pre-literacy and literacy skills as readily and incidentally as their peers do, needing direct instruction and opportunities for repetition to consolidate newly acquired skills. Young children with dyslexia normally experience difficulties with the development of pre-literacy skills, being perceived by some educators not as children with literacy difficulties but as children who are not ready to learn. There is a move, however, away from this view to explore children's attitudes, disposition and behaviour with regard to learning, the context within which learning takes place, the effectiveness of teaching methods and the wider societal and cultural factors that shape their literacy development.

Dyslexia is a contentious concept meaning different things to different people. Parents and teachers talk about special educational needs and dyslexia in ways that suggest that dyslexia has an implicit meaning difficult to define and agree upon. This is particularly true for young children whose developmental needs change rapidly with the boundaries between typical and atypical development being less clear. Issues regarding dyslexia in young learners are complex, and the limited research on early predictors of dyslexia and reading difficulties does not make things easier. Recognising early indicators of dyslexia is a grey area within which early years staff strive to meet children's learning needs effectively.

## Defining dyslexia

In this section, I present various definitions of dyslexia to delineate its characteristics and place them in the wider SEN context. Before discussing what dyslexia entails, I would like to present the frequently used term SEN and differentiate it from 'special needs'.

Special Educational Needs (SEN) is an all-encompassing term that reflects diversity in children's learning and developmental profiles. Specifically, it refers to pupils' characteristics that can be grouped into the following four sub-areas: cognitive and learning difficulties; emotional, behavioural and social difficulties; communication and interaction difficulties; and sensory and/or physical difficulties (DfES, 2001). These areas are not clear-cut in that there is diversity within each group. There is also a great deal of overlapping with boundaries that are 'cross-cutting, fluid and shifting' (Thomas, 1997: 103). SEN was introduced as a legally defined term by the Education Act 1981 following the advice from the Warnock Committee (DfES, 1978). Prior to 1981, the focus was on identifying and providing for 'handicapped individuals'.

Special Educational Needs refers to the learning difficulties experienced by children in an educational setting, making them eligible for educational provision. On the other hand, special needs is not a legally defined term, referring to the needs displayed by children whose cultural, linguistic and social backgrounds and experiences are different from those of the majority children. Using these terms interchangeably has serious ethical and practical implications in that children who experience special needs may not necessarily have SEN. Special needs tend to refer to social phenomena that may be shared by children from similar social-cultural and linguistic backgrounds and, thus, they are distinct from individual experiences of learning difficulties which underlie SEN (Frederickson and Cline, 2002). Confusion of the terms SEN and special needs is likely to result in perceiving children from minority ethnic and linguistic backgrounds as having learning and/or language difficulties and, as a result, planning and implementing educational support that may not be relevant or developmentally appropriate for them. Also, confusion of these concepts may lead to low expectations, inappropriate attributions for academic success and failure, discrimination and, potentially, racism. Differentiating between special needs and SEN can be particularly tricky when teaching young children whose literacy difficulties may be due to their limited language and other developmental needs.

There is no single definition that encapsulates dyslexia. Different definitions of dyslexia reflect a wide range of theories and perspectives that have been put forward to explain literacy difficulties, as well as the public's understanding of dyslexia and its influence on educational policy, research and practice. The following definitions intend to give you a flavour of the diversity inherent in dyslexia.

The Orton Dyslexia Society definition describes dyslexia as a specific learning difficulty that affects phonological development, word decoding and word recognition, reading, spelling and writing. It states that dyslexia should not be the outcome of limited educational/social opportunities or other conditions (e.g. sensory impairment). In other words, poor learning progress should not be attributed to children's school and home-based learning experiences or any other aspects of their social context. The assumption of this definition is that children experience learning difficulties despite adequate educational exposure and appropriate teaching. The fact that this definition excludes social-cultural factors has consequences with respect to identifying and assessing dyslexia in young children from minority linguistic and social-cultural backgrounds (Cline and Shamsi, 2000) (see Chapter 2 for a detailed discussion).

According to the Orton Society definition, learning difficulties are seen as being unexpected given the child's ability and age, pointing to a mismatch between ability and academic performance. This understanding of dyslexia has influenced its assessment and diagnosis by introducing the discrepancy criterion to guide diagnosis. This approach to diagnosis has been the most prevalent in the UK and the USA for many decades. Over the years, the validity of using the discrepancy criterion has been criticised heavily and the use of intelligence scores (IQ scores) has been questioned extensively by theorists and practitioners alike (e.g. Stanovich, 1996).

The Orton Society definition is exclusionary in that it states what dyslexia is not rather what it is. Over the last decades, there has been a shift in terms of moving from exclusionary definitions of dyslexia to more inclusive ones. A recent report by the DECP of the British Psychological Society (BPS) on Dyslexia, Literacy and Psychological Assessment has proposed the following working definition of dyslexia:

> Dyslexia is evident when accurate and fluent word reading and/or spelling develops very incompletely or with great difficulty. This focuses on literacy learning at the 'word level' and implies that the problem is severe and persistent despite appropriate learning opportunities. It provides the basis for a staged approach to assessment through teaching.
>
> (BPS, 1999: 5)

According to the BPS working definition, dyslexia refers to difficulties in accuracy and fluency of reading and spelling at the word level. This definition does not rely on the discrepancy criterion in terms of a marked difference between aptitude and performance, nor does it refer to intelligence scores. Also, the BPS working definition leaves open the possibility that a number of children might have acquired satisfactory literacy skills if appropriate pre-school and initial teaching experiences and learning opportunities were given (this is the learning opportunities hypothesis). The shift in our understanding regarding the origins of literacy difficulties and their implications places an increasing emphasis on the importance of early years teaching and learning as a way of supporting young learners to make a good start.

Another definition that draws direct links between assessment and teaching is the one stated in the Code of Practice for SEN. The Code of Practice is a non-statutory document produced by the Department for Education and Skills (DfES, 2001) and provides practical advice on meeting children's special educational needs. The Code of Practice defines special educational needs as the result of a child having learning difficulties, including dyslexia. Under Section 312 of the 1996 Act, children with learning difficulties are those who

(a) have a significantly greater difficulty in learning than the majority of children of the same age; or
(b) have a disability which prevents or hinders them from making use of educational facilities of a kind generally provided for children of the same age in schools within the area of the LEA; or
(c) are under compulsory school age and fall within the definition at (a) or (b) above or would do so if special educational provision was not made for them.

According to the Code of Practice, special educational provision means:

(a) for children of two or over, educational provision which is additional to, or otherwise different from, the educational provision made generally for children of their age in schools maintained by the LEA, other than special schools, in the area;
(b) for children under two, educational provision of any kind (para 1.3).

Interestingly, different understandings of dyslexia, as reflected in these definitions, have influenced teaching and classroom practice in different ways. There is a growing consensus among professionals that defining dyslexia based on phonological difficulties, short-term memory difficulties, speed of information processing and reading/ spelling difficulties at the word level has a clear theoretical basis (Frederickson and Cline, 2002). An implicit understanding in all these definitions is that children with dyslexia do not learn at the same rate, style and manner as their peers. Specifically, they may find it difficult to memorise and retrieve information, understand the sounds of language, link sounds to letters and manipulate them accordingly, process information at speed and develop reading and writing skills at the level expected for their age and educational opportunities. Anyone teaching young children with dyslexia should take into account the variety of perspectives on dyslexia and their implications for teaching and learning.

## Early characteristics of dyslexia

A number of hypotheses have been put forward to explain dyslexia and its underlying characteristics (Frederickson and Cline, 2002). Researchers from diverse backgrounds have suggested that difficulties with phonological development (e.g. Snowling, 1995; Stanovich, 1988, 1996; Siegel, 1990), visual processing (e.g. Stein, 1989; Wilkins, 2003), working memory (e.g. Rack, 1994) and information processing speed (e.g. Wolf, 1991), either in combination or alone, are likely to explain dyslexia.

### Phonological development and dyslexia

As I will discuss in Chapter 2, young children with dyslexia are likely to display difficulties with certain aspects of language, phonology, which is the awareness of the sounds that comprise words, in particular. Phonological difficulties are usually evident in poor understanding and recognition of rhymes, weaknesses in the segmentation and blending of sounds in terms of recognising the first and final sound in a word, not pronouncing words correctly, i.e. f/th 'fing' as opposed to 'thing', and difficulties making sound–letter correspondences. Phonological difficulties are also related to poor sound discrimination and speech that some children display when they start going to school. Phonological difficulties become evident in children from as early as the third year of age, and in some cases, even earlier.

The phonological deficit hypothesis explains dyslexia by focusing on difficulties with phonological processing in terms of making links between sounds and letters (phoneme and grapheme) and developing phoneme awareness, i.e. being able to tell which sound comes at the beginning or the middle of a word and blend/segment sounds properly during word decoding. A large body of research suggests that phonological difficulties constitute the core characteristic of dyslexia (Siegel, 1990; Snowling, 1995; Stanovich, 1996). Others warn against adopting a definition for dyslexia based on phonological development alone, in that some children with dyslexia may not present phonological difficulties. Specifically, Frederickson and Frith (1998) looked at a group of children with dyslexia with serious reading difficulties and identified a subgroup, i.e. 20% of children in the original group, who showed no evidence of phonological difficulties despite their difficulties with reading. This suggests that children with dyslexia do not constitute a homogeneous group, stressing the need to also consider other factors/characteristics of dyslexia, namely visual processing and working memory, and the ability to process information at speed.

### *Visual dyslexia*

Lovegrove and his colleagues examined the link between visual processing and dyslexia, in that difficulties have been identified with the ability to process visual information in children with dyslexia (Lovegrove *et al.*, 1990). Specifically, these researchers demonstrated that children with dyslexia displayed sensitivity for detecting flicker. Visual difficulties have also been suggested by Stein who found that adults with dyslexia show difficulties associated with eye movement during reading with regard to the ability to fixate their eyes on words for as long as it is required (Stein, 1989). Consequently, difficulties with processing visual information (e.g. letters, number, symbols) are likely to affect reading and writing, especially in young children who tend to rely on the visual properties of letters and numbers to recognise them.

As young children move into reception year, reading individual letters and words becomes particularly important. During reading, some children may experience visual stress and complain about headaches, sore red eyes, brightness of page and distortion of letters and lines. Children with difficulties processing visual information often feel that words are 'moving' or being 'muddled up' during reading, experiencing signs of visual strain.

Wilkins argues that visual stress is experienced by a surprisingly large number of children, i.e. 5 to 20% of typically developing children (2003). He describes visual stress in terms of movement of print with words breaking up or joining up, letters moving around and with the spaces between words appearing and disappearing randomly. Also, blurring print is another symptom of visual stress in terms of letters changing size, letters doubling or extra letters appearing at the end of words, letters fading or becoming darker, and patterns appearing on paper. Visual stress is linked with headaches, nausea or dizziness.

Early years staff catering for young children with a wide range of needs are most likely to observe certain behaviours or physical signs that suggest visual strain during reading. As Wilkins points out, children who experience a form of visual distress tend to move close to or away from the page, constantly changing their head position, rub their eyes and blink excessively and use their finger to track, often losing their position in text. As a result, these children tire quickly and display sore red eyes. There are some simple questions that you, as a practitioner, can ask children who display these behaviours and their parents, to explore the possibility of visual stress. These may include:

- Do the letters stay still or move on the page?
- Do the letters appear fuzzy or are they clear?
- Are the words too close together or far enough apart?
- Does the colour of the print change with letters appearing darker or less dark?
- Do you have to use your finger when you read?
- Does it hurt your eyes looking at letters/words? and
- Do you have a headache after looking at letters or words? (Wilkins, 2003: 16, 17).

These questions can help you identify children who may require a specialist optometrist test and benefit from the use of colour overlays for reading. You and other classroom staff are in a position to raise these concerns with children's parents and make a referral to an optometrist who is a specialist in measuring visual function, above and beyond a conventional eye examination. In the UK, a referral is normally done through the general practitioner. During an optometrist testing, different overlays may be used to determine the colour that appears to be suitable to reduce visual strain in children.

### Working memory, processing speed and dyslexia

Difficulties with short-term memory and sequential memory are observed when children struggle to learn the alphabet, the times tables or remember the names of familiar objects (Rapid Automatising Naming Task), especially when put under time pressure. Research in this area has found children with dyslexia to present difficulties with processing linguistic and non-linguistic information at speed. In an early study by Denckla and Rudel (1976) children with dyslexia often experienced difficulties with 'rapid automatised naming' of common objects or colours. Specifically, children were shown pictures of familiar objects (e.g. toys, household items) and were asked to name them as fast as they could. It was found that children with dyslexia had difficulties retrieving the words fast. Along this line of research, Wolf (1991) established that early difficulties with naming letters and numbers at speed predict later problems in reading. Wolf and Bowers (1999) suggested the 'double deficit' hypothesis to explain difficulties in both phonological skills and speed of information processing, typically displayed by children with dyslexia. The double deficit hypothesis suggests that children with dyslexia experience a range of difficulties including problems with phonology, visual processing and memory.

### Motor co-ordination skills

Other researchers have found an association between dyslexia and difficulties with motor skills, especially in young children (Nicolson and Fawcett, 2000; Rudel, 1985). Specifically, difficulties with certain motor functions, such as leg balance, walking backwards or the ability to recognise shapes traced on skin when blindfolded, toe tapping and successive opposition of fingers and thumbs have been found to correlate with dyslexia. Also, difficulties with gross and fine motor skills, sequencing and processing information at speed are likely to put obstacles in children's copying from blackboard, handwriting, engaging in serial/sequential tasks (e.g. learning times tables and the alphabet) and engaging in visual analysis (e.g. discriminating a letter from a word or a sentence, finding their place when reading). With this in mind, for young children with dyslexia, classroom strategies should focus on recognising shapes (e.g. circle, rectangle), learning words that indicate spatial relationships (e.g. under, up, around, near, far), playing games that support spatial awareness (e.g. puzzles) and alleviating confusion with left and right.

Clearly, researchers from different disciplines and backgrounds have identified a range of characteristics or pointers of dyslexia, acknowledging the diversity and complexity of this area of need and suggesting that a sole approach to understanding dyslexia and supporting children's learning is not adequate. Many of the characteristics of dyslexia described here appear at the early stages of children's development. Thus, early identification and acknowledgement of potential literacy difficulties has important practical implications with regard to the effectiveness of early intervention.

**Case study**

The following case study illustrates a number of characteristics or early pointers likely to be evident in young children with dyslexia.

Jamie is a five-year old boy who, according to his mother, experiences difficulties with orientation, appearing unco-ordinated and clumsy. He bumps into furniture and household objects and gets into accidents very often. At school, Jamie is in trouble with his peers in that he interferes with their games, interrupts them when they talk and can never follow the rules of the games. The teacher comments that Jamie lacks social skills, in that he does not know when to take his turn in a conversation, nor can he apply negotiation strategies when faced with a conflict situation. He gets easily excitable and has difficulties controlling his behaviour, especially at the playground. In classroom, he has difficulties following instructions and getting used to the daily classroom routine (transition, putting his stuff and clothes away, etc.). The class teacher has to make eye contact with him to ensure that he is aware he is addressed. In terms of language development, his speech is not very clear and he has difficulties grasping the phonics, i.e. sounds of language, and recognising some of the letters of the alphabet. He also displays difficulties with recognising and sequencing numbers. Jamie's handwriting is particularly poor in terms of letter form/size and line directionality, with his pencil grip being awkward. Also, copying from the board is difficult in that, compared to his peers, it takes him much longer with his writing often being inaccurate and untidy.

## Gifted young children with dyslexia

Young children's developmental and learning profiles are diverse, presenting areas of strength and weakness. This diversity is particularly evident in able children who underachieve academically. Able children with learning difficulties, including dyslexia, present a challenge to educators and parents in that it is difficult for them to reconcile the dual nature of high ability combined with learning and/or emotional/behavioural difficulties. Able young children with dyslexia are likely to experience difficulties with short-term memory and hand–eye co-ordination, as well as frustration emanating from not being able to show their good intellect in their academic work. Motor skills, especially fine motor skills, often lag behind cognitive abilities, particularly in gifted pre-school children (Webb and Kleine, 1993). These children may know what they want to do, e.g. construct, draw; however, poor motor skills do not allow them to achieve their goals, resulting in frustration and emotional outbursts. Regarding their self-esteem, gifted young children with dyslexia tend to be highly self-critical in that they evaluate themselves on what they are unable to do, rather than on their substantial abilities, impacting on their sense of self-worth and emotional maturity and adjustment (Whitmore and Maker, 1985).

Early years staff should be aware of certain characteristics that normally raise the alarm for possible learning difficulties in able young children. These include children:

- presenting potential without necessarily being motivated
- showing a marked discrepancy between oral and written language

- having a low self-esteem and being self-critical
- displaying a short attention span and
- disguising their ability to alleviate peer pressure.

Able young children with dyslexia display learning difficulties as well as problems with concentration in terms of a poorly sustained attention in classroom and the playground, and are more active and restless than typical children, having difficulties adhering to rules and regulations (Barkley, 1990). With this group of children, it is not easy to determine whether limited concentration is related to dyslexia or to giftedness. Webb (1993) observed gifted children displaying poor attention, boredom, daydreaming and low tolerance for repetitive tasks and learning activities that are less challenging intellectually.

With regard to the social and emotional development of able pre-schoolers, they need reassurance and the time and space to talk about their feelings. In the context of circle time and peer-mediated activities (see Chapters 2 and 3), gifted young children with dyslexia are encouraged to display social and emotional intelligence by taking others' perspective and inferring about their thoughts and emotional states and showing good leadership qualities and good language and communication skills.

## Classroom support: pre-literacy strategies

Practical guidance to support young children, like Jamie, who display characteristics of dyslexia, namely phonological difficulties, slow information processing, difficulties with motor skills and sequential memory, should be geared towards strategies that support orientation, phonological skills, short-term memory, spatial awareness and sequencing. These strategies can take place in early years classroom in that dyslexia-related characteristics are likely to be present from early on.

Browne (1998) argues for the implementation of a developmentally appropriate curriculum to maximise opportunities for young children to develop the necessary attitudes and disposition for literacy development. She specifically referred to opportunities to

- engage in purposeful and relevant learning activities
- gain real understanding of new concepts
- discover and learn through active experimentation
- develop motivation and interest in what is learned
- become confident learners and
- acquire positive dispositions towards lifetime learning (1998: 9).

Also, certain environmental changes are likely to facilitate concentration and task persistence in young children with dyslexia. Classroom arrangements and strategies that are likely to support children's attention include:

- To seat children with dyslexia and concentration difficulties close to you and away from distracting environmental stimuli such as doors, windows, or pencil sharpener;
- To make direct eye contact frequently with them and call their names before asking them questions or engaging them in an activity;
- To assure that their working space is clear of distractions, and present only one task at a time;
- To position them among attentive, well-focused pupils;

- To use physical contact (e.g. a hand on the shoulder), in addition to eye contact, to promote attention to task;
- To provide positive feedback and incentives to decrease distractibility (e.g. points for being attentive and on task, individual charts, stickers, etc.);
- To praise them when they are focused and attentive by commenting on it.
- To use certain signals and cues that have been arranged with them to help focus their attention; and
- To structure reading and writing so that they can be carried out in pairs or small groups. For maximal involvement and attention, co-operative learning is an ideal strategy for keeping pupils engaged and participating.

The implementation of pre-literacy strategies starts from the family. Family-centred interventions have been found to be effective, with the parents playing an important role in maximising their children's ability and encouraging their involvement in pre-literacy activities. Ezell, Justice and Parsons suggested ways of ensuring that family-centred interventions meet children's emergent literacy skills successfully.

Specifically, they stated that the main thrust of family-centred interventions should be on building partnerships between early years practitioners, e.g. nursery/reception teachers and parents in order to

- give parents the information they need about their children's development;
- provide them with instructional plans and materials for shared literacy activities at home; and
- train them through immediate feedback to encourage their children's emergent literacy skills, especially with children who, in addition to dyslexia, present language and communication difficulties (2000).

With regard to the last point, Ezell and her colleagues developed a training scheme aimed at increasing parents' verbal and non-verbal references to print, such as commenting on print and pointing to letters during shared reading with children to maximise early book-reading interactions and stimulate children's emergent literacy. As an early years practitioner, it is important to think about the distinctive features and demands of language (speaking and listening skills) during reading and writing. You should identify aspects of your instructional strategies and activities (e.g. language use, presentation of instructions) that may place obstacles to learning for pupils with dyslexia, and through differentiation, tailor-made teaching to make the 'perfect fit' between the curriculum/teaching strategies and pupils' learning needs. This is not an easy undertaking, in that you need to develop an insight into the pupils' learning styles and needs, use assessment to identify their needs and modify your classroom practices to support pupils' literacy. For young children with dyslexia, differentiation has achieved its aims when their learning is supported in terms of not only knowing more but also wanting to know more. This is important for motivating children with dyslexia who are likely to experience frustration and display reduced motivation and low self-esteem.

When applying differentiation in reception, Y1 or Y2 classes, it is helpful to think in terms of processes, lesson content, resources and outcome. Bills and Brooks described a number of differentiation strategies including differentiation by 'task', 'resource', 'time', 'support' and 'outcome' (2004: 79, 80). With these strategies in mind, you may differentiate by

- *Task* – In terms of modifying its content and setting different goals. For example, during writing, you may provide pupils with dyslexia with a set of letters to be used to facilitate spelling and writing, whereas pupils without dyslexia are expected to engage in writing letters and forming simple words without providing them with a list.
- *Resource* – In terms of engaging children in the same task but use different resources to meet their diverse needs. This is a particularly useful differentiation strategy especially during multi-sensory teaching whereas different modalities are used to support learning. For example, during reading, pupils with dyslexia may listen to a book on tape or watch a video about the topic, circumventing reading altogether.
- *Time* – In this case the goals of the task and the procedure remain the same but the amount of time allowed for task completion differs, with pupils with dyslexia having more time to complete a task. During copying, children with dyslexia process and transfer the letters into paper much slower than their peers, perhaps due to their difficulties with short-term memory and sequencing.
- *Support* – Group or 1:1 work provided by you or a learning support assistant is required to support children with dyslexia on a particular aspect they find it difficult, e.g. phonics, letter recognition, times tables.
- *Outcome* – In this case the task remains the same but the outcome is differentiated. For example, during writing, pupils with dyslexia who find writing challenging may produce a drawing instead. Or during reading, children with dyslexia may listen to a story or a tape recording of a book and then may be asked comprehension questions orally.

Although differentiation is considered to be an important aspect of the National Curriculum, it is a challenge to apply it, especially within the constraints of the early years curriculum. For young children with dyslexia, the content and learning goals should be differentiated and expanded to include activity-oriented learning and play, as well as strategies geared towards the development of language and social skills. Early years learning outcomes should also expand beyond formal literacy skills, namely, recognising letters, alphabet reciting, to embrace peer interactions, communication, self-esteem, social adjustment and emotional maturity.

## Summary

In this chapter, I discussed various definitions of dyslexia in an attempt to delineate its early characteristics and indicators. A number of hypotheses have been put forward to describe and explain the difficulties experienced by children with dyslexia, including phonological difficulties, poor short-term memory for both auditory and visual information, slow pace of information processing and difficulties with visual processing. Also, I discussed the learning and social needs of able children with dyslexia who, despite their very good ability, underachieve academically, further contributing to the paradoxical nature of young children's learning and development. Finally, I presented pre-literacy strategies in the context of differentiation to support young children with dyslexia in early years classrooms.

# Chapter 2

# Language and communication in young children with dyslexia

## Introduction

Currently, there is an increasing concern with regard to the language skills, such as speaking, listening and using language as a social tool, children bring in early years settings. A survey by the Basic Skills Agency (2003) shows that almost two-thirds of the teachers questioned feel that there is a gradual deterioration in the level of language competence of young children. This is a serious concern in the face of extensive research suggesting strong links between language development, the ability to access the curriculum and social skills development (e.g. Adams, 1990; Catts and Kamhi, 1999; Dockrell and Lindsay, 2001; Hartas and Donahue, 1997; Hartas and Warner, 2000).

Language and communication skills constitute an important aspect of children's early literacy development. Increasing research evidence suggests a co-existence between dyslexia and language difficulties, phonological difficulties in particular. With this in mind, this chapter focuses on language development and language difficulties in the context of dyslexia. Language difficulties in young children may be missed easily, especially if they are subtle and/or co-exist with other conditions, e.g. dyslexia. Another factor that makes it harder to define competence in language and communication skills in young children is the variability in the rate, style and manner they acquire language. The learning needs of children with language difficulties are both diverse and complex and, thus, they should be alleviated to enable them to access the curriculum and acquire literacy and numeracy skills (Riley *et al.*, 2004). Young children need good language skills to follow instructions, participate in classroom discussions, engage in peer interactions and express their ideas, feelings and thoughts.

As I will discuss in the next chapter, the development of language skills is likely to remove obstacles towards social-emotional development by giving children the means to express feelings, articulate concerns and externalise frustration in a socially appropriate manner. During interactions and observations, reception and nursery staff can identify early indicators of difficulties in some or all aspects of language, namely phonology/ sounds, grammar and syntax, meaning and use of language. Understanding the linguistic, social and psychological aspects of language development will also enable you, as a practitioner, to map young children's receptive and expressive language needs and plan a structured programme for language support.

## Emergent literacy and language skills

Numerous studies have established that young children with language difficulties find oral language and emergent literacy very challenging, pointing to a strong interdependence between oral language acquisition and literacy development (e.g. Boudreau and Hedberg, 1999; Chaney, 1992; Gillam and Johnston, 1985; Snow *et al.*, 1998). This interdependence may explain why children with language and communication difficulties demonstrate restricted emergent literacy skills compared to their peers with typical language skills (Ezell *et al.*, 2000). It is thus argued that supporting the development of language skills (both comprehension and language use) in young children, especially those who display early characteristics of dyslexia, can pay dividends in supporting their learning.

Language permeates every aspect of the curriculum, further pointing to the interdependence between literacy and language skills. Specifically, receptive language skills are required for children to understand teachers' questions, explanation, requests, instructions, descriptions and organisation of classroom activities. Expressive language skills are needed for children to express thoughts and feelings, build and maintain personal relationships with both adults and peers, formulate ideas and engage in problem solving.

Despite research evidence suggesting a strong link between language and literacy, Riley and her colleagues argue that language development receives little attention within the NLS in that it does not include specific objectives with regard to linguistic and communicative competence (Riley *et al.*, 2004). They also stressed that in the intervention strategies designed to support language development, language should not be viewed as discrete skills that need to be taught, but as a 'complex area of cognitive functioning' that develops through rich and meaningful social interactions (Riley *et al.*, 2004: 671).

## EAL young children with dyslexia: language difficulties or language difference?

As an early years practitioner, you will most certainly encounter young EAL pupils. EAL children constitute a very heterogeneous group and thus generalisations about their literacy and language development are not always accurate, nor are they helpful for classroom practice. There are many factors, such as social and cultural background/ experiences and their current family circumstances, to be considered before making judgements about EAL pupils' linguistic development and literacy.

Young children from minority ethnic and linguistic backgrounds may experience learning difficulties, requiring additional educational provision due to the fact that they speak English as an additional language. It is also possible that they display learning difficulties in their first language. In the first case, children are likely to experience learning difficulties (special needs) as a result of their limited proficiency in English due to their minority linguistic background. In the second case, they are likely to experience learning difficulties in both first and additional language pointing to special educational needs.

As I discussed in the previous chapter, the distinction between the terms SEN and special needs is supported by a legislative framework, specifically stating that 'a child must not be regarded as having a learning difficulty solely because the language or medium of communication of the home is different from the language he or she is taught' (Department for Education and Employment 1996, Section 312). Regarding young children with dyslexia from minority linguistic and/or ethnic backgrounds with language difficulties in English or their native language or both, differentiating between SEN and special needs is not easy. When it is not clear whether children display SEN or special needs, you, as a practitioner, should investigate certain factors such as

- the length of the time they have been in the UK;
- the language(s) spoken at home, the family circumstances (e.g. parents who are asylum seekers/refugees, or professional parents who work and/or study in the UK);
- the value placed by their family and the surrounding community on learning English (is learning English seen as a form of cultural subjugation or as an empowering act?); and
- children's prior linguistic experiences.

Moreover, you need to explore the extent to which schools or early years settings value EAL children's culture and language and respond to their differences effectively. Considering children's language development within their social-cultural context is crucial for engaging in a responsive pedagogy. Au and Kawakami (1994) reported that culturally relevant instruction in terms of acknowledging pupils' home language and patterns of social interaction, and structuring classroom interactions in ways that are consistent with the pupils' home values and beliefs, increase learning opportunities in pupils from diverse backgrounds.

The development of language and literacy in EAL young children is influenced by social, cultural and political factors, including the status that is given to the child's first/ native language at school and the wider community, the conversational patterns at home and, in many cases, the lack of continuity between the languages spoken at home and those spoken at school (Pang and Kamil, 2004). Hornberger did a comparative analysis of bilingualism and biliteracy in Puerto Rican and Cambodian communities in Philadelphia, and established that EAL pupils need to be supported along the

- macro–micro continuum (political and socio-economic factors which support the development and acceptance of biliteracy);
- monolingual–bilingual continuum (the use of both languages in school and community);
- oral–literate continuum (the use and support of oral and written language by the school and community) (1992: 210).

Lack of support along these continua was found to have a negative effect on children's use of their first language and, consequently, on their literacy development. In Chapter 5, I will discuss ways of supporting EAL young children to achieve oral proficiency in English and develop literacy.

## Classroom guidance

To place the following classroom strategies in a real-life context, I would like to discuss a case study of a young child who experiences both language and literacy difficulties.

Jack is a five-year-old pupil who presents difficulties acquiring literacy and numeracy skills. At the nursery, his teachers noted that he rarely speaks and that he does not use symbolic play either. By the time he entered reception he was exhibiting certain limitations in his language with regard to providing answers to simple questions and following instructions, signing nursery rhymes and reciting/recognising the alphabet. His speech is not clear and he forms simple, two-word sentences only. When he is upset or anxious he tends to scream, kick and poke other children or grab their things. At times, he appears sad and withdrawn, and rarely plays with other children, interacting with younger children mainly. Although his parents are not involved actively in his education, they have raised concerns about his lack of academic progress, language difficulties and his not easily manageable behaviour. Academically, he presents difficulties with the acquisition of literacy skills such as recognising letters and numbers, linking sounds to letters and deciphering simple words.

## Supporting children with dyslexia to become 'linguistic beings'

Early year practitioners need to have a good understanding of the basic aspects and principles of language and communication development in young children, as well as the importance of the child–caregiver interaction and its impact on both language and social-emotional development (Jarvis and Lamb, 2001). Specifically, early years practitioners should

- strive to minimise rigid patterns of interaction, be responsive to children and follow children's lead during conversations;
- use words and phrases consistently, and draw links between language and children's experiences so that language has meaning and familiarity;
- avoid fragmented interactions by giving time and space to interact on an one-to-one basis with children and get to know them well;
- provide children with linguistic and contextual support and prepare the conversational ground by giving them background information before starting discussing a specific topic, explaining the rules of a game, talking about the listeners' intentions and making links with prior events and experiences that children are familiar with; and
- work collaboratively with parents and other early year practitioners, and observe each others' practice through the development of peer mentoring.

Working closely with parents is important in that young children's early language experiences are shaped mainly in the context of their families. There is evidence that involving parents to support young children's emergent literacy skills has proven successful, particularly with those with language difficulties (Dale *et al.*, 1996). Enhancing children's early language skills can be achieved by encouraging and supporting parents to take a lead role in facilitating their children's language during everyday interactions. Many early language intervention programmes rely to a great extent on parental involvement, by training parents to engage in shared reading with their children, give praise and ask open-ended questions during social interactions (Ezell *et al.*, 2000; Whitehurst *et al.*,

1988). An interesting intervention study in this area was conducted by Hockenberger *et al.* (1999) where parents, as the primary intervention agents, engaged their children with language difficulties in shared reading and discussions surrounding the text (see 'extended text' in Chapter 5) to encourage the use and understanding of language.

For young children to become competent linguistic beings, caregivers and classroom staff should support them through modelling and opportunities for social interactions to:

- use functional language, e.g. request information or an object, protest, inform, comment;
- use language as a social tool, e.g. greet, apologise, negotiate, apply strategies to carry out a conversation, e.g. turn-taking, repair when a communicative breakdown occurs, change and maintain a topic of conversation;
- display communicative intent, e.g. sharing information with another person and respond to others' communicative attempts;
- take the speakers' or listeners' perspective by understanding their goals, intentions and beliefs; and
- use gestures or body language when the talker and listener share the same physical context. For example, if a child says, 'Give this from over there' then this can be interpreted accurately only if the listener is in the same room with the speaker. If this is not the case, children should be encouraged to use language more explicitly.

The development of language skills depends upon opportunity, time and contextual support (Searcy and Medaows, 1994). Early years classrooms are conducive towards supporting language in that they are not as highly structured as most primary school classrooms, offering many opportunities for social interaction and language use. Specifically, circle time and peer-mediated activities provide the structure to teach young children a wide range of language and communication skills through storytelling, role playing, modelling and coaching. Early years staff, such as reception teachers and learning support assistants, can support young children with the acquisition of these communicative skills by

- defining words in context and giving examples to ensure that children understand word meaning and how meaning changes depending on the situation;
- providing visual cues, e.g. smiling/sad faces to teach emotion words;
- explaining implied messages, as well as the use of figurative language, e.g. metaphors;
- acknowledging cultural differences and their effects on verbal and non-verbal communication (e.g. avoiding eye contact, gestures);
- speaking slowly and clearly;
- using storytelling and role playing to model language use; and, last but not least,
- taking into consideration children's emotions in that how they feel is likely to affect their use of language.

Regarding language development in EAL young children who also display dyslexia, it is useful to evaluate their starting point with learning English or any other additional language(s). This is not easy in that language is a complex behaviour and thus subtle language difficulties may be missed, especially if the child appears to be chatty and use language in a superficial manner. Cummins (1984) distinguishes between Basic

Interpersonal Communication Skills (BICS) and Cognitive Achievement Language Proficiency (CALP) when evaluating children's additional language(s). Specifically, Cummins claims that children who converse with their peers during social interactions in the playground may not have the linguistic competence required to use language to access the curriculum or participate in classroom discussions.

Among EAL pupils, a particularly vulnerable group is children from refugee families, newly arrived in the UK, seeking political asylum. These families face serious challenges ranging from persecution in their own countries to anxiety waiting for decisions about their refugee status. In these circumstances, young children are likely to be traumatised given that their social and linguistic experiences are constructed in the context of their family. Furthermore, the cultural shock from facing new societal systems and norms, feelings of being displaced and, in some cases, open hostility and racism, all contributing to difficulties learning an additional language and developing literacy skills.

There are simple ways to support newly arrived EAL young children in your classroom. You should

- approach them and their family, through an interpreter or liaison officer;
- locate and deploy support from bilingual staff;
- help pupils access bilingual materials (e.g. dictionaries, books, videos, audio tapes), depending on whether they are literate in their first language;
- encourage them to use their first language during classroom discussions, in playground and in written work. This is likely to support their self-esteem, knowing that their culture and language are valued;
- give time and space to newly arrived children to 'tune in' the classroom. Classrooms are overwhelming environments and even more so for children who are not familiar with the routines, the social interaction styles and the cultural references made by people who share a common code of behaviour;
- become a positive model of language behaviour yourself by demonstrating language and communication skills during play and other social interactions;
- form groups with children who speak their own language, if there is more than one bi- or multi-lingual child speaking the same first language, and alternate the groups with English speaking children so they have the chance to be exposed to both languages; and
- use visual aids and demonstrate activities and tasks with many examples, avoiding lengthy verbal instructions.

## Classroom strategies for language and literacy development

In this section, I present instructional strategies that have a dual function in terms of supporting children with language and literacy difficulties. These strategies can be implemented during circle time, group collaborative activities, storytelling or unstructured activities. During circle time, you and other adults in the classroom can implement effective remedial language strategies. Circle time is a structure with what Searcy and Medaows (1994) described as 'fluid boundaries', encouraging children to move freely from one activity or group to another and test their newly acquired language/communication skills. This is particularly beneficial for pupils who are shy and/or socially withdrawn in that, during circle time, they are given the opportunity to contribute to classroom discussions and model appropriate language use before encountering any formal classroom structures in primary school (a detailed account of circle time is given in the next chapter).

During peer collaborative activities and other group interactions, language skills are practised and consolidated. Young children are likely to find group discussions less intimidating, enabling them to talk about their feelings, share ideas with others and build on previous contributions, test important language skills such as turn-taking, problem solving and negotiation strategies, engage in perspective taking, show empathy and tell stories. Storytelling has been found to facilitate language in terms of teaching young children conversational turn-taking, providing clarification and elaborating on their and others' responses, showing communicative intent and using appropriate vocabulary in the context of social interactions (Westby, 1999). Moreover, direct discussions about story characters' perspective and their interactions support pupils' ability to take others' perspectives and talk about emotion. For pupils with dyslexia who present good oral language, storytelling is an effective way of enhancing their literacy skills.

To support young children with widespread speech, language and communication difficulties you and other classroom staff may apply differentiation techniques by modifying teaching to focus on developing expressive and receptive language and communication (e.g. listening, comprehending and responding) during circle-time discussions and group interactions. You may also create opportunities for social interactions across settings (e.g. classroom, playground) by fostering conversations through constructions, role playing and structured activities that require children to explain the steps and the outcome with sufficient detail in order for others to re-create it. A number of suggestions by Gross include:

- Using computer software involving two children; one child creates and prints a picture and then gives instructions to another child in the keyboard to re-create the image without seeing it.
- Using a box with materials (varying in colour, texture, shape) with one child choosing a specific material and describing it to the other child accurately enough so he/she can identify the piece, again, without seeing it.
- Having one child to tape record instructions on how to make a particular construction and then have a group of children trying to follow the instructions (2002; paraphrased).

More strategies targeting the development of expressive language skills include:

- Provide story tapes and ask children to listen to them and re-create what they hear. Children with language difficulties are provided with some key words to facilitate recall and story structure. Also, story books with pictures provide a good visual aid to assist children with story recall.
- Ask children to talk about their own experiences, e.g. family trips or holidays, or events and situations that can relate personally.
- Encourage children to express their interests that are meaningful to them. Partnerships with parents can be very useful to find out about children's interests and the social interactions they have with their family members and the immediate community.
- Encourage children to ask questions for clarification, obtaining extra information and eliciting others' ideas in a group.

- Develop a routine for children to greet each other by providing some key words and phrases for those with difficulties and encouraging them to repeat them.
- Facilitate the formulation of responses to others' questions in a group by providing some key words and phrases.
- Use the Literacy Hour structure (details in Chapter 5) to carry out sentence-level work by focusing on verbs, plural, possessives, prepositions (in, on, under, behind) and tenses.
- Encourage children, especially those with word retrieval difficulties, to express themselves by providing them with forced alternatives, if necessary, and then asking them to elaborate on their answer.
- Model and encourage the use of 'What', 'When', 'How' and 'Why' questions.
- Expand vocabulary through the use of a dictionary, or visual maps in which children take a word and write other words that seem to relate to it to consolidate the learning of new words.
- Illustrate that words can have many meanings, through the use of riddles, word games and jokes.

You may also encounter children, such as Jack in the case study described in this chapter, whose speech is not clear. According to Gross (2002), you and family members should

- encourage children to use gesture or drawings instead of words;
- give them time to offer several versions of what they are trying to say;
- use forced alternatives, not 'yes' or 'no' answers;
- set up opportunities for social interactions and encourage them to talk about a shared experience;
- speak slowly and clearly to children in an attempt to model good speaking skills; and
- encourage the use of body language (e.g. gestures).

Some children may present difficulties understanding language, hindering their functioning in the classroom, especially their understanding of verbal instructions. You and other classroom staff and family members should

- get children's attention first, before you speak call their name and/or establish eye contact;
- avoid speaking out of context, by establishing a background to the conversation;
- place children in a position that can help them pick up what is happening by watching other children;
- use pictures and modelling through demonstrations of the task at hand;
- break long and complicated instructions or sentences into manageable components (task analysis) and ask them to take a step at a time;
- ask children to recite what you said, preferably in their own words; and
- use consistent vocabulary.

## Language as a social tool

Strategies to support the development of the social use of language (both receptive and expressive) should focus on teaching skills required for making requests, engaging in problem solving, greeting and initiating conversation, taking turns and taking into account the listeners' needs (Audet and Tankersley, 1999). To support children with communication difficulties interact with adults and peers, you may practice with them conversational skills such as making requests for attention, objects, action, assistance, information and clarification. These include:

- understanding non-verbal cues in a given social situation/context, e.g. raising hand, pointing, eye contact;
- developing expressive vocabulary (see above);
- comprehending utterances, implicit and explicit meanings;
- using language to talk about their own thinking/understanding in order to request more information or clarification (know what they know and be able to express that);
- showing awareness of the social-cultural norms of a setting;
- using verbal and non-verbal means to obtain attention from listeners;
- practising with formulating responses to questions; and
- raising awareness of changes in conversational topics and respond accordingly.

Also, turn-taking skills are crucial for knowing when it is the children's turn to contribute to classroom discussions. Circle time, with the use of a toy that is passed around or visual aids, provides a facilitative structure to support young children with turn-taking. Finally, being able to manage a conversational topic is important for young children to communicate effectively. Topic management is a complex communicative skill, requiring linguistic and social knowledge to initiate a topic, maintain it for as long as it is required and change it when it is appropriate. It also requires adequate expressive and receptive vocabulary, understanding of non-verbal cues, skills to repair when a communicative breakdown occurs, clarification when necessary, awareness of the listeners' needs and background information. For young children with language difficulties, topic management poses many challenges, requiring time and opportunity to develop social and linguistic knowledge.

## Summary

Young children with dyslexia who also experience language and communication difficulties present complex needs and serious challenges for early years staff. Supporting children with dyslexia and language difficulties, as well as those whose English is an additional language, to become competent linguistic beings, capable of accessing the curriculum and interacting with peers is not an easy undertaking. You, as a practitioner, are required to accommodate multiple facets of diversity and become aware of the socio-political and cultural factors that shape children's linguistic experiences and literacy. As I will discuss in the next chapter, literacy, language and social-emotional development are interlinked, suggesting the need for integrated approaches towards classroom support.

# Chapter 3

# Pastoral care in young children with dyslexia

## Introduction

When we think about children with dyslexia, what comes immediately to mind is difficulties with learning and literacy usually manifested as underachievement in their academic work. There is, however, another, less obvious and acknowledged side to dyslexia, that of behavioural/social and emotional difficulties that are usually triggered by the frustration and low self-esteem that children with dyslexia typically experience. The social and emotional consequences of dyslexia have been neglected despite accumulating evidence suggesting a strong link between dyslexia and difficulties with regard to social interactions and emotional maturity (e.g. Kendall *et al.*, 1990).

Some young children with dyslexia are vulnerable socially, especially those whose learning difficulties are compounded with restricted expressive and receptive language. In order for these children to be successfully included in the mainstream, they need support that integrates language, literacy and social skills development. This is important in that there is evidence to suggest that social difficulties experienced by children with SEN pose serious barriers to successful inclusion (Allen and Tarnowski, 1989; Frederickson and Cline, 2002).

This chapter focuses on the social-emotional aspects of learning and language development in young children with dyslexia. Its main premise is that language and social-emotional development are interconnected, and that difficulties with social adjustment, ability to express feelings, self-confidence and self-esteem are likely to have a long-term impact on learning and academic performance. With this in mind, understanding the relationship between social-emotional development, language and learning in young children with dyslexia has important practical implications for integrating intervention goals that target language, literacy and behaviour.

There are numerous intervention programmes aiming at promoting social competence and pro-social behaviour, especially with primary school children (e.g. Roffey *et al.*, 1994). There is also an agreement among practitioners to incorporate social, language and communication skills training into the early years pastoral curriculum. Overcoming communication difficulties that are likely to hamper social interactions and emotional adjustment, learning how to make and retain friends and recognising and dealing with negative feelings and peer rejection are thought to promote social inclusion and improve schools' social climate and ethos (Allen and Tarnowski, 1989).

## Social-emotional difficulties and dyslexia

Recently, an increasing emphasis is placed on social skills and emotional maturity for social adjustment and learning. The growing interest in the relationship between social-emotional difficulties and learning in young children with dyslexia in particular has been prompted by concerns expressed by teachers and parents about the impact of learning difficulties on dyslexic pupils' social and emotional development. Many parents of children with dyslexia agree that the social-emotional consequences of dyslexia, such as low self-esteem and lack of self-confidence, are more severe and long lasting than are difficulties with literacy *per se*. The relationship between social-emotional and learning difficulties is complex and cannot be easily untangled. For practical reasons, however, it would be helpful for early years practitioners to differentiate between children with emotional/behavioural difficulties, such as hyperactivity, withdrawal, who consequently develop learning problems, and those who have learning problems and subsequently experience social-emotional difficulties, including tantrums, clinging behaviour, low self-esteem, anxiety or frustration.

Research evidence suggests that children with dyslexia are usually met with academic failure, resulting in being unmotivated and demoralised, unresponsive to and withdrawn from school-related activities and peer interactions and, ultimately, experiencing social-emotional difficulties (Allen and Tarnowski, 1989; Seligman *et al.*, 1984). Children with dyslexia are also likely to be perceived less favourably by their classmates, leading to difficulties with peer interactions and, potentially, with social adjustment. Conversely, children with social-emotional difficulties exhibit poor concentration, short attention span, anxiety and lack of motivation, experiencing difficulties with learning. Also, children who are shy and socially withdrawn report low self-esteem, make negative self-statements and experience hopelessness and helplessness in that they take less responsibility for academic outcomes, resulting in poor academic performance (Pearl *et al.*, 1980).

Dyslexia is an invisible disability and its characteristics are not immediately obvious and recognisable to teachers and parents. Consequently, judgements about children with dyslexia tend to be subjective and somewhat misleading. Children with dyslexia are likely to be described as being lazy, immature and disruptive, lacking interest and motivation and the ability to concentrate. Although it is not easy to ascertain whether learning or social-emotional difficulties are the primary condition, in the majority of children, behavioural/emotional difficulties are triggered by problems with learning and literacy. As I discussed in the previous chapter, children with dyslexia are also likely to display difficulties with the use and understanding of language, which may also explain their difficulties with peer interactions, pro-social behaviour and social skills development.

### Social-emotional skills: what do they entail?

There is not a commonly agreed definition of social skills in that there are not any absolute criteria as to what constitutes acceptable or desirable behaviour across cultures and societal norms. Parents and teachers from diverse social and ethnic backgrounds attribute different value and importance to social skills, and have different understandings of the features/behaviours that reflect emotional maturity in children. According to Caldarella and Merrell (1997), social skills underlie positive peer relationships, and are normally expressed in terms of taking others' perspective and showing empathy, using language as a social tool and engaging in social problem solving. Self-monitoring skills or the ability to moderate and manage one's own behaviour, compliance skills with regard to following rules and norms/expectations and assertion skills in terms of being independent are also thought to contribute to children's social adjustment.

Prizant and Wetherby's definition of social-emotional development refers to the ability to experience, regulate and express a range of emotions, establish positive relationships with others and develop a sense of self and a social identity (1990). This definition acknowledges the important role that language plays in children's emotional expression and peer interactions. In the social skills literature, it is widely recognised that young children with language and communication difficulties are at high risk for developing social-emotional difficulties and vice versa (e.g. Hartas and Patrikakou, 1997; Rice, 1993; Rogers, 1991; Westby, 1999). It has been found that as many as 50–70% of children with language difficulties display social-emotional or behavioural difficulties (Baker and Cantwell, 1991; Prizant and Wetherby, 1990). Conversely, children with emotional difficulties such as shyness and withdrawal experience problems with the production of coherent speech (Prizant, 1999). For example, shy children are likely to produce a statement 'I did not start it. He took it and I pushed him and then I ran here' (1999: 298). In this statement the listener does not know what it was started, who took what, how many people were involved and where or why they ran. Understandably, children whose expressive language suffers are likely to have difficulties relating to their peers and forming meaningful relationships.

Moreover, children with a combination of language and social and emotional difficulties are likely to experience difficulties with planning and regulating behaviour in order to attain a goal. According to Welsh and Pennington, moderating behaviour involves the ability to defer a response to a later more appropriate time, develop a strategic plan of action, has a picture of the task in mind and sequences the actions required to complete it (1988).

Using language as a social tool during interactions requires more than a mere knowledge of the structure of language and a good vocabulary. Children need to have the social knowledge to enable them to 'tune in' to a social situation. Social knowledge involves understanding others' point of view, thoughts, beliefs and wishes by observing their behaviour and the social cues available. Being aware of others' thoughts and feelings is what Baron-Cohen (1995) refers to as 'theory of mind'. For children, theory of mind is a way of representing mental states, such as thinking, believing, knowing, guessing or deceiving, to enable them to use the words that map these mental states accurately. Once young children are able to represent mental states they are able to identify, understand and talk about their and others' emotions, as well as engage in discussions and express views about social and moral situations.

Westby (1999) has provided a thorough account with regard to three-, four- and five-year-old children's understanding and representation of mental states. Specifically, by the third year of age, children understand that they see the world differently from how other people see it, and experience emotional situations differently. They also recognise the difference between real and imaginary objects/events and use words such as remember, think or know. By the fourth and fifth year of age, children understand others' desires and beliefs and that different people can have different points of view and understandings of what they see and how others feel. They already understand peoples' beliefs and desires are connected with their actions and, most importantly, they can use language to influence others. By reception, children are able to understand that the same situations can produce different feelings in different people, using language to reflect on events and emotions.

With regard to understanding and responding to emotions, pre-schoolers are able to match emotion words such as happy, sad or angry, to faces. They know that hugging is right and hitting or hurting is wrong, and are able to predict that if a child or a puppet receives a toy that do not want they will cry or get angry. Pre-school children can also make direct links between emotions, language and specific events/experiences. For example they connect the feeling of being happy with a birthday party, and the feeling of being sad with losing their favourite toy, and can use simple emotion words consistently (Michalson and Lewis, 1985, as cited in Westby, 1999).

Children from a very young age are expected to talk about feelings, be aware of others' feelings and thoughts and form relationships with peers and adults. Undoubtedly, both expressive and receptive language skills play a paramount role in identifying and talking about emotions and relating socially to others. Young pupils with dyslexia co-existing with language and communication difficulties are likely to face multiple challenges, ranging from understanding and contributing to discussions in the classroom to forming relationships with peers. Early years staff should be aware of the complexity of these difficulties and also realise that what sometimes appears as non-responsiveness, lack of social reciprocity and reduced motivation to participate in discussions and problem solving tasks may be a manifestation of limited conversational skills.

The following case study illustrates the profile of a young child with dyslexia who also experiences language and social-emotional difficulties (low self-esteem).

Andrew is a four-year old who was born prematurely. His development has been normal except for speech and language skills. His speech is not very clear and he gets teased occasionally by his peers. He also presents problems expressing his feelings and gets easily frustrated. His teacher said that he often appears 'disengaged' and withdrawn in the classroom. When he is asked to work on a specific task he looks what the other children are doing and then he follows them. When interacting with other children, he tends to grab their things instead of asking for them politely. When an argument arises he remains silent or just repeats what he wants in very simple sentences (one- or two-word sentences) loudly. In the playground, he is often on his own. He has made a good progress during circle time, especially with regard to learning when it is his turn to talk and how to ask politely when he wants something. His teacher is working on nurturing his self-esteem by giving him responsibilities and encouraging him to talk about his interests. Also, he has been supported in learning how to use emotion vocabulary and to recognise emotions in others with the help of pictures and other visual aids. Although he is making good progress with regard to his social and emotional development, his language production and comprehension still lag behind, impacting on his pre-literacy and literacy. Academically, he experiences difficulties with phonological development and, subsequently, letter and word recognition. Andrew receives support focusing on rhymes recognition through songs and flash cards.

In this case, taking an integrated approach to intervention is important in terms of supporting diverse yet inter-related areas of Andrew's development, namely social-emotional skills, expressive and receptive language skills and literacy. The following sections focus on ways of transforming classrooms into caring environments capable of supporting children academically and socially.

## Creating caring classrooms

Creating what Gross (2002) describes as a 'caring classroom' can be particularly challenging especially in today's crowded classrooms where an increasing emphasis is placed
on performance indicators and measurable academic results. However, there are certain
activities (e.g. modelling and coaching), patterns of interaction between adults and pupils
and among pupils themselves and structures (e.g. classroom physical environment and
instructional demands) that have the potential to meet pupils' social and emotional needs,
minimising potential obstacles to learning (Audet and Tankersley, 1999).

Early years classrooms should be organised in ways that are less threatening and
more 'fluid', where children are allowed to interact with each other and with the staff,
and become independent in their decisions about accessing materials and collaborating
with others. Also, it is crucial that positive relationships between young children and
staff are built. This can be achieved with adults

- encouraging children to engage in problem solving actively and offering praises
  and rewards;
- explaining the rules and the consequences of breaking them, presenting discipline
  not as a punishment but as an act of responsibility;
- modelling pro-social behaviour and feelings of empathy;
- recognising and dealing with signs of emotional distress; and
- assisting children in forming friendships.

Furthermore, caring classrooms encourage children to talk about their feelings and
understand how others feel. Structures such as circle time, peer-mediated activities and
nurture groups have been found to support social and emotional literacy by encouraging
young children to explore and understand emotional and social responses and develop
the communicative and social skills necessary for active participation and independent
learning. Specifically such skills include:

- Classroom skills, including listening, concentrating, following instructions.
- Communication skills such as turn-taking, sensitivity to the listener's needs,
  providing background information, requesting for clarification and greeting.
- Friendship making/sustaining skills, such as joining a group, initiating and maintaining conversation.
- Emotional skills in terms of understanding and using affect-denoting words,
  showing affection and recognising others' emotions.
- Social problem-solving skills in terms of resolving a conflict situation, dealing with
  emotionally charged situations, e.g. bullying, and presenting alternative solutions.

## Enhancing language and social-emotional literacy

The revised Code of Practice (DfES, 2001) places an emphasis on the development of
social and emotional skills by supporting children to adjust to school expectations and
routines and acquire the skills necessary for engaging in positive interactions with peers
and adults. Specifically, it states that pupils who experience social difficulties need help:

- with the development of social competence and emotional maturity;
- in adjusting to school expectations and routines; and

- in acquiring the skills of positive interaction with peers and adults (DfES, 2001; para. 7.60).

Young children rely on language skills to develop relationships and learn from others. There is strong evidence that language and social-emotional difficulties are linked with learning/academic difficulties in pre-school children, making the need for language intervention more pressing than ever (Aram and Hall, 1989; Dockrell and Lindsay, 2001; Sabornie, 1991). Early identification of language and social-emotional difficulties in children with dyslexia is crucial for the implementation of classroom strategies that integrate literacy and social-emotional goals.

You, as a nursery or reception staff, are likely to face many challenges catering for pupils who experience low self-esteem and self-confidence, a reduced sense of self-worth, lack of motivation, shyness, difficulties forming friendships, limited linguistic input (especially immigrant/refugee children) and, possibly, social disapproval from peers. Classroom strategies to enhance language and social-emotional literacy in children with dyslexia require you to set appropriate goals, modify your teaching styles and put systems in place to remove obstacles to learning. These strategies can take place in the context of circle time and peer-mediated activities, as well as during modelling and coaching to ensure effective teaching for young children with dyslexia who find linguistic and social interactions particularly demanding.

Classroom strategies to support children with language, social and literacy difficulties include:

- Arrange seating with children being in small groups close to the teacher or learning support assistants.
- Provide each pupil with their own space where they feel secure and confident.
- Separate pupils with a history of negative interactions from one another.
- Develop structures within which social interactions and storytelling are supported (e.g. circle time).
- Set areas where unstructured activities, e.g. play, are encouraged.
- Provide verbal and non-verbal support during transition (e.g. certain words to indicate lining up, gestures and other non-verbal signals) to minimise confusion.
- Explain classroom rules and use simple vocabulary in a consistent manner.
- Use visual aids (e.g. pictures) to support identification and expression of emotions.
- Encourage children to give praise to each other, and engage them in relationship talk, reflection and sharing of their emotional experiences.
- Explain the demands of tasks by using simple words and provide repetition in a calm voice.
- Ensure that instructions are understood before asking children to follow them by maintaining eye contact with pupils and using demonstration techniques. And
- Encourage collaborative learning for children to practice language and social skills (e.g. peer-mediated activities).

The complex needs of children with dyslexia can be met by integrating linguistic, academic and social-emotional goals via differentiation during circle time and peer-mediated activities, as well as other classroom structures supporting self-esteem, friendship formation and the building of emotional bonds.

## Circle time

Circle time and peer-mediated activities are likely to support young children's learning, language and social-emotional development. Circle time has gained recognition as an educational technique that creates a warmer, caring and inclusive ethos, ultimately helping children develop a sense of affiliation (Lang, 1998). Circle time is an increasingly popular method in the UK schools for promoting confidence, self-knowledge, communication and self-esteem, and equal opportunities especially with pupils with SEN.

In circle time, everyone sits in a circle preferably at the same level creating a sense of equality. The results from a study in Sweden on the educational and social content of circle time stated that it contributes to the development of personal identity, fosters democratic values and enhances social skills (Reich, 1994). Teaching language and social skills within a circle-time pedagogy is likely to help young children with dyslexia feel that they are part of what is going on and thus to be genuinely integrated. It also gives them the opportunity to make statements about themselves, providing meaningful feedback by encouraging them to identify positive qualities and give negative feedback in a constructive manner.

During circle time, you may look for signs of emotional distress in young children in terms of clinging behaviour or tantrums, and explore a wide range of emotional issues through drama and role-playing. Although circle-time activities can have different aims the philosophy is the same, being a positive early years setting where everyone is listened to and has equal rights and opportunities (Wolfendale, 1997). Mosley (1996) highlighted the contribution of circle time to pupils who display negative behaviours, such as disruption, clingingness and aggression, or withdrawal and shyness, and suffer from low self-esteem, lacking positive social models. Circle-time interactions support the re-building of self-esteem in children by creating an empathic, powerful and controlled self, and help them achieve attainable targets regarding behavioural standards in the classroom and the playground.

Furthermore, Mosley and Tew (1999) recognised that, during circle time, teams are built to support the development of social and communicative skills, sustain friendships, and encourage personal and social responsibility by understanding rules and moral values. Finally, stories and personal narratives are used as a tool for language and social-emotional development to enable young children with dyslexia make personal and meaningful connections.

## Peer mediation

Another instructional technique that can be implemented in parallel with circle time is peer mediation. Peer-mediated interactions have been found to enhance interpersonal skills particularly in children with language and behavioural difficulties (Audet and Tankersley, 1999; Chan, 1996). In early years settings, you may form collaborative groups and assign tasks with well-specified goals and expectations to support social problem-solving skills by providing direct language support, verbalising strategies to resolve conflict and disagreement, and developing and carrying out a plan of action.

With respect to children's social development, peer mediation has been found to support the emergence and application of negotiation, communicative and problem-solving skills to resolve a conflict situation (Carriedo and Alonso-Tapia, 1996). Peer-mediated activities involve expressive and receptive language and pose social demands. For pupils to be part of a group, they need to comprehend the vocabulary used, retain directions and rules in their short-term memory as they engage in activities, formulate appropriate responses and understand the social dynamics of their interactions with others. Young children with dyslexia, who also experience language and behavioural difficulties, usually find these interactions very demanding, resulting in frustration and, possibly, withdrawal.

Regarding literacy development, peer-mediated activities provide the instructional frame to support reading by promoting acquisition, maintenance and generalisation of learned strategies (Green *et al.*, 1988). It is widely accepted that language plays a major role in literacy, e.g. learning the alphabet, decoding/recognising words (Au, 1992; Catts and Hugh, 1996). Thus, during peer-mediated activities, children can be taught phonics and how sounds relate to letters and encouraged to attempt rhyming tasks to support reading.

Peer-mediated activities are central to transforming early years settings into caring environments with reduced opportunities for bullying and other violations of children's rights. Pupils with behavioural, social and emotional difficulties are likely to benefit from peer mediation in terms of anger management, pro-social skills development and empathy, i.e. taking into account others' feelings. Moreover, peer-mediated interactions can help pupils

- manage their behaviour and emotions by setting realistic demands
- develop clear and predictable structures of rewards and sanctions
- value and respect the contribution of others
- engage in both independent and collective work
- build self-esteem and become confident as learners, and
- explore different ways of learning within an environment they feel safe.

Circle time and peer-mediated activities have the potential to assist children in practising newly acquired social, language and literacy skills and proving feedback and positive reinforcement from you and peers. Specifically, children are taught how to take conversational turns, make comments to other children to initiate conversation and use 'conversational starters' presented visually to talk about their social encounters with siblings at home and children at school. You, other classroom staff and parents should encourage children to talk about their games along the lines of what went well, what problems they encountered and what they did to resolve them. Finally, in the context of circle time and peer-mediated activities, children are given many opportunities to build emotional bonds, make friends, talk about feelings and build their self-esteem and self-confidence.

### Building emotional bonds

It is widely known that language and social-emotional development flourish in the context of strong, intimate relationships between children and their caregivers and educators. In early years classrooms, timetable and financial constraints, key staff's patterns of work and, finally, lack of employment stability for early years practitioners are likely to disrupt the development of emotional attachment and strong relationships between children and early years practitioners. Although it is important to ensure that the staff/pupil ratio is good, having the correct number of adults available does not necessarily ensure that strong and meaningful relationships are built, 'unless the organisation of the setting ensures regular occasions when concentrated attention is given by a particular caregiver to a particular child' (Goldschmied and Jackson, 1996: 11).

One way of supporting young dyslexic children's learning, self-confidence and self-esteem is through the establishment of positive personal relationships that model pro-social attitudes with you, family members and peers. Most importantly, as Alder and Sandor (1990) argue, we need to ensure that young children with complex special educational needs, such as dyslexia co-existing with emotional/behavioural/social difficulties and language difficulties, are not asked to participate in activities for which are not adequately prepared and supported. Emotionally, facilitating learning and encouraging engagement in play and other activities for enjoyment offer a sense of accomplishment and progression.

Forming close relationships with young children is a balancing act for many early years staff who do not want to be seen as 'replacing' the parents in any way, nor do they wish to become too emotionally involved with a child who will be moving on to another provision at a later stage (Jarvis and Lamb, 2001). Although the relationship between children and their educators is important, children's family is the basis for language and social-emotional development. Thus, understanding the influence of family structures and routines on children's development will enable you, as a practitioner, to learn from and incorporate these influences in your classroom strategies.

### Making friends

Early years classrooms and activities, such as circle time, are ideal to encourage children to talk, share toys and materials, show empathy and socialise through play. The importance of positive interactions during early years is stressed in a study by Duck (1991) which found that the relationships formed during the nursery school years are likely to affect children's future social interactions in terms of peer acceptance/rejection, popularity and ability to enter groups and make friends. Puttalaz and Gottman (1981) also found that unpopular, aggressive, or socially withdrawn children tend to perform poorly at school and have difficulty forming adult relationships in later life. It appears that poor social skills at an early stage are likely to affect both social interactions and learning.

### Talking about feelings

Being able to identify, name and distinguish between feelings is a key to developing emotional literacy (Dowling, 2001; Dunn, 1993; Goleman, 1995). Helping children build an emotional vocabulary is crucial for social-emotional development in that they can use linguistic means to express negative feelings or frustration. As Smith (2002) argues, learning how to handle emotions is particularly important to minimise antisocial or inappropriate behaviour, especially for children with social-emotional difficulties and poor communication skills. With this in mind, introducing Smith's 'Box Full of Feelings' into the nursery curriculum is likely to support children understand the four basic emotions, namely happiness, sadness, anger and fear.

The 'Box Full of Feelings' framework can be used to teach young children how to identify and talk about their feelings. Specifically, each emotion is presented and discussed in depth by showing children a large picture. An introduction takes place at three stages to help children to identify the emotion. First, the children are asked individually 'How do you think this little girl is feeling?' and are given time to think about their response. Second, when everyone gives a response, children's attention is drawn to a body posture with the view of raising their awareness of body language associated with the emotion discussed. The third stage of this process is making a link between the emotion and their personal experience by asking the questions 'What makes you feel happy? What makes you feel sad? What makes you angry? Have you ever been scared?' (Smith, 2002: 142).

Finally, in your classroom, you may support children's expressions of emotions by teaching them to engage in an 'experiential dialogue' in terms of encouraging them to have respect and care for others (Laevers and Van Sanden, 1995). Experiential dialogues are thought to support emotional growth, in that children are encouraged to talk about how they feel, and, more importantly, how the other person feels when encountering a conflict situation.

### Building self-esteem

The way in which self-esteem boosting programmes are introduced to children is absolutely crucial to determine their success (Lawrence, 1996). During play, storytelling activities or circle time, children's contribution is recorded and then all children listen to it to feel that their contribution is acknowledged. This process supports self-esteem and language skills, as well as self-confidence by sharing individual contributions with the whole group. For children who are shy and socially withdrawn, you may support their self-esteem by, for example, having a toy (e.g. doll, teddy bear) passing around to signal when to take their turn and speak to the group. This is an effective tool for turn-taking enabling children to participate in a conversation without interrupting others. Similarly, role playing with the use of a puppet is a good way for children to learn about feelings and ways of expressing them.

These approaches towards supporting emotional and social development can certainly be embedded in the circle time or peer-mediation activities. However, for children who require more direct, focused and hands-on support with social skills development, modelling and coaching may be a better choice.

### Modelling and coaching

A range of intervention approaches including modelling, coaching and social problem solving are available to support children's social skills development (Frederickson and Cline, 2002). These approaches are particularly relevant to the social needs of pre-school children in that they are hands-on, actively engaging children who may be shy or withdrawn, and can be implemented in the context of circle time and peer-mediated activities. In your classroom or the playground, you most likely use praise and other rewards as the means of acknowledging behaviour that is socially appropriate. For example, giving attention is a reward for a child who asks politely another child for help or a toy. Praise and rewards are effective as long as they are consistent with you being constantly aware of good behaviour occurring in order to reward it. Although it is important to reward good behaviour when it happens, it is equally crucial to make it happen by actively modelling it and helping children to achieve it through coaching and opportunities for pro-social behaviour.

Modelling involves a step-by-step demonstration of the appropriate behaviour and it may involve 'talk aloud' in order to explicate the steps. For example, you or a socially competent child may demonstrate how to enter a group and initiate conversation with peers. This may focus on using language to attract the group's attention, initiate and maintain a conversational topic that is relevant to the group interests, greet the children in the group, take others' perspective and show empathy by using emotion vocabulary appropriately.

For some children demonstrating what needs to be done to achieve social goals is sufficient. Very young children, however, may require more direct support, provided step by step to demonstrate a particular social interaction (Frederickson and Cline, 2002). For these children, coaching is an effective strategy allowing you to explain to them what to do while they are involved in doing it.

The following example illustrates the use of modelling and coaching to support young children with language, literacy and social difficulties to develop the social skills necessary to approach a peer who appears to be distressed, take his/her perspective and show empathy through the use of emotion vocabulary. During modelling and coaching, you may demonstrate the steps, explain what needs to be done and the order it needs to be done, and encourage children to practice the steps in a role-play situation. For this example, I use Oden's framework (1986) for coaching to provide a step-by-step support to a child (child A) attempting to approach a distressed peer (child B).

*Step 1*: Explain to child A how we recognise emotions in others and the things that we look for to understand when someone is happy, sad, upset or angry. Then explain the meaning of relevant emotion words, e.g. upset, unhappy, scared, and make the link between emotion words and how child B is likely to feel. Talk about feasible ways of finding out what makes child B distressed, by supporting the child A to make links between events and emotions.

*Step 2*: Practice the use of emotion words and give examples/scenarios by asking child A to identify and describe the emotions present. Also, practice phrases that child A can use to make child B feel better, as well as social problem-solving skills in terms of providing alternative solutions to resolve the problem.

*Step 3*: Help child A to generate and express solutions that are likely to alleviate his/her classmate's distress and make plans about how to approach child B.

*Step 4*: Encourage child A to practice the newly learned social skills during role-play. Ask child A how he/she feels, in that understanding his/her emotional reaction is important to support child A to show empathy to child B.

*Step 5*: Hold a revision session with child A where you ask questions about what child A did and the helpfulness of the strategies suggested by you. If things have gone well encourage child A to use the same strategies next time; if not, reflect on what went wrong and present alternative strategies.

A step-by-step demonstration can be effective for children who need direct input. It is important, however, to ensure that children have developed social knowledge and the capacity for empathy necessary for social interactions, and that the social skills learnt during coaching can be successfully transferred into different contexts and situations.

## Summary

In this chapter, I presented a less acknowledged aspect of dyslexia, that of social and emotional difficulties in young children with literacy difficulties. Recently, there has been a growing interest in the development of social skills in children in general, and in those with dyslexia in particular. A large body of research has stressed the importance of good social skills for peer acceptance, positive social interactions, social adjustment and learning. Classroom strategies were suggested, ranging from structuring the classroom environment in ways that support the development of language and social skills (circle time) to engaging in peer-mediated interactions, modelling, coaching and classroom differentiation techniques.

# Chapter 4

# Identification and assessment of learning and development in early years

## Introduction

Early identification of developmental and learning difficulties has always been a high priority for research, policy and practice in education. Early years practitioners are well placed to raise concerns and identify learning difficulties experienced by young children. It is widely accepted that the earlier learning difficulties, e.g. dyslexia, are identified the more likely it is for parents and educators to minimise their impact on young children's learning and social-emotional development.

Although nobody denies the logic of this, the reality of identifying and diagnosing potential learning difficulties is more complex than what it appears to be. This is particularly true for young children whose rate of development varies hugely, with no clear-cut boundaries between typical and atypical development. Young children's behaviour and learning are more variable than when they are older and, certain factors such as a mismatch between their early learning experiences with their families' and schools' expectations and culture are likely to affect their learning significantly.

Moreover, the lack of devices and procedures capable of providing rigorous and accurate information about young children's functioning hinders identification further. Many educational researchers and practitioners have raised concerns with regard to the appropriateness of current assessment devices and, most importantly, debated the notion of 'diagnosing' young children's educational needs through the use of standardised instruments. Lindsay (2004) argues for taking a 'systemic approach' to meeting the diverse learning needs of young children in terms of obtaining useful information that will enable teachers and other classroom staff to modify their teaching and re-adjust the learning goals and outcomes.

If we are to take an interactional approach towards assessment, we need to assess the characteristics of the individual learner as well as the learning environment. According to the Code of Practice, 'the assessment should always be fourfold: It should focus on the child's learning characteristics, the learning environment that the school is providing for the child, the task and the teaching style' (DfES, 2001, para. 5.6). This statement is understood by taking four distinct approaches to assessment and focusing on the learner, the teaching programme, the 'zone of potential development' and the learning environment (Cline, 1992). Delineating young children's educational and developmental needs is crucial before making decisions about provision. Assessment lies in the heart of identification and diagnosis; however, as Frederickson and Cline (2002) argue, assessment becomes a particularly challenging task when the children involved are young.

## Assessment: another aspect of teaching?

Assessment is an important aspect of teaching that should 'not be regarded as a single event but as a continuous process' (DfES, 2001, para 5.11). The Code of Practice (DfES, 2001) stresses the importance of taking an evidence-based approach to teaching and learning by accumulating data to demonstrate pupils' progress and make decisions about teaching. The Code of Practice also provides the framework for teachers and other practitioners to assess and identify areas of need through the use of screening assessment tools. Formal diagnostic assessments are time-consuming, involving the use of complex skills that normally teachers and other classroom staff have not been trained to apply. Interestingly, in recent years, the use of technology has offered teachers the opportunity to engage in diagnostic assessments, e.g. computer-based assessment, without investing a lot of time. A computer-based assessment refers to any 'psychological assessment that involves the use of digital technology to collect, process and report the results of that assessment' (BPS, 1999: 1).

Despite the increasing use of technology-supported assessments and the ongoing refinement of assessment devices, there has been a great deal of fragmentation in the provision of educational services for young children (Pugh, 1988). This is partly due to the lack of consensus among professionals regarding assessment approaches and early identification procedures, and partly due to the limited awareness about children's learning and developmental needs. Regarding the latter, children with severe or complex difficulties are identified earlier than are children with less 'objective' and visible difficulties. This is changing gradually with early years education becoming more prescriptive through the implementation of the early years curriculum and ofsted inspection, resulting in monitoring children's progress during the foundation stage of education (three to five years). In this climate, early years practitioners are expected to be confident to deal with assessment and identification of children who present learning and other developmental difficulties in a highly skilled manner. This is not easy, especially when considering issues regarding the

- developmental appropriateness of current standardised assessments;
- lack of professional agreement on what constitutes slow development and what atypical development or difficulty is;
- lack of norms for early years;
- diversity in methods of assessment (qualitative/quantitative) and their link to provision;
- validity and meaningfulness of assessment results in terms of informing classroom practice; and
- complexity of language and social skills, and the difficulty assessing them without reducing them into discrete skills.

Although standardised tests present a number of limitations, if used and interpreted properly and in conjunction with qualitative approaches, they provide useful information

about young children's development and learning. Early years assessment should include both qualitative and quantitative strands. A quantitative assessment normally involves the use of standardised tests to assess children's strengths and weaknesses in, for example, memory, verbal and perceptual/visual skills and motor skills. Qualitative approaches involving observation and interviews are more developmentally appropriate for young children and likely to yield valid and meaningful results to inform teaching. Specifically, observations of children's functioning in different contexts and discussions with family members are likely to yield rich information about language, social-emotional development and emergent literacy. As a nursery and reception staff, you are well placed to collect qualitative information through your everyday observations of and interactions with children, and liaison with their parents.

## Foundation Stage Profile

With regard to assessing young children, the statutory baseline assessment scheme at school entry has changed to the Foundation Stage Profile (FSP) implemented at the end of the foundation stage (the end of reception year) (QCA/DfES, 2003). The FSP is regarded to be inclusive in that it provides guidance and practical examples about assessment procedures relating to children with a wide range of strengths and needs. Its scope is to assess all six areas of learning as stated in the Early Learning Goals: namely personal, social and emotional development; communication, language and literacy; mathematical development; knowledge and understanding of the world; physical development; and creative development.

Assessing young children at the end of the Foundation Stage should rely on accumulating evidence from your interactions with and observations of them. An interesting aspect of the FSP is that it assesses the progress children make by taking into consideration their individual profile and needs. Specifically, children's demonstration of having attained a particular item in the scale is interpreted in the context of their strengths and weaknesses. According to the FSP, assessing communication, language and social skills and literacy will require you to look for certain behaviours that are indicative of children's ability to

- listen and respond
- initiate communication with others
- use language to monitor behaviour and guide actions
- listen to stories, songs or rhymes
- use language during role-playing and
- use language to organise thinking and feelings, showing an awareness of listeners' needs.

The Code of Practice (DfES, 2001) advises on involving parents at every stage of their children's assessment and evaluation. During the initial qualitative assessment, you should obtain background information regarding the areas of functioning as stated in the FSP through formal or informal discussions with parents and carers (a detailed discussion on home–school partnerships is found in Chapter 7). You may ask parents about

- the onset of language, to clarify whether the child was late at learning to talk, where late means not talking two- to three-word sentences by the age of two years, or not using reasonably correct language by the age of three;

- their views of their children's language development and whether there are other languages spoken at home;
- whether their children have any difficulty learning nursery rhymes and songs;
- the overall medical history of their children, i.e. anything unusual beyond the normal childhood illnesses such as frequent ear infections, hearing or eyesight problems;
- their children's interests and things they are good at;
- any unusual family circumstances that possibly have affected their children's development (e.g. bereavement, separation);
- whether there are any close family members who experience literacy difficulties; and
- their children's self-esteem and self-confidence with regard to learning and social interactions.

## Qualitative assessment: dyslexia, language and social development

For young children with dyslexia, assessment should focus on delineating their strengths and needs with regard to pre-literacy and literacy skills, communication, language, and personal, social and emotional development. As I discussed in previous chapters, children with dyslexia are, in addition to literacy difficulties, likely to display social-emotional difficulties and language and communication problems. The FSP provides the framework to delineate all these areas by taking an integrated approach to assessment to enable you and other classroom staff to plan teaching and learning effectively.

Assessing young children's development and learning on a continuum of abilities and needs requires you to identify early pointers of dyslexia in terms of reduced pre-literacy behaviours, language and speech difficulties, poor co-ordination and concentration, limited social skills and signs of emotional immaturity. Using the FSP framework, you may assess young children's

- emergent or pre-literacy skills by focusing on behaviours that are associated with learning such as following instructions and routines, remaining on task for any length of time, organising their work, e.g. locating and obtaining the materials required, clearing up space to work, collaborating with other children on a joint task, working independently and being confident to ask for help if required;
- language and communication in terms of understanding and manipulating sounds (phonological skills) and, most importantly, taking turns, speaking and listening, storytelling, using emotion words and initiating and maintaining conversational topics;
- emotional maturity, in terms of their ability to take others' perspective, show empathy (feelings of sympathy) and talk about emotional situations (e.g. death of a pet) appropriately;
- social and interpersonal skills in the way they approach other children to play with, form friendships and resolve conflict when it arises;
- self-esteem and sense of self-worth, in terms of talking about things they are good at, taking pride at their work, responding well to praise and rewards and feeling confident to express their opinions in a group; and
- auditory and sequential memory by asking them to recall digits forward and backward to understand how children memorise and organise information in their short-term memory. Short-term memory difficulties are typically manifested when children have difficulties following multi-step instructions or directions.

### Pre-literacy and literacy

During the initial assessment of young children, it is important to take into consideration the settling period as well as their prior learning experiences in the context of their family and immediate community. Assessment should be an integral part of effective early years practice, enabling you and other classroom staff to focus positively on children's individual strengths, learning styles and social-emotional development. To this end, the goal of assessment is to help you gain a thorough understanding of young children's functioning and build trusting relationships with them and their family. Children should be assessed in a range of natural contexts and with regard to their individual experiences and achievements, and use a range of procedures and sources of evidence, including observation, discussions with family members, developmental history, work samples, language samples to gather information.

With regard to pre-literacy, e.g. phonological development, and formal literacy skills, e.g. reading and writing, you may look for behaviours and attitudes that indicate pupils' ability to

- tune with rhyming activities
- link sounds and letters, and recognise the initial and final sounds in words
- use phonic knowledge to read and write simple words
- develop an interest in books
- know that print conveys meaning
- show an understanding of the elements of stories such as the main character, sequence of events and the beginning and the end of a story
- experiment with mark making, sometimes giving meaning to marks
- hold the pencil effectively to form recognisable letters
- trace shapes adequately
- recognise the name of numbers and
- communicate meaning through phrases and simple sentences.

Implementing the FSP to delineate children's skills is also useful for gifted young children, EAL children and children with hearing difficulties. As I discussed in previous chapters, these groups of children are likely to experience difficulties with literacy, language and social-emotional development.

Identifying children with high ability who also present literacy difficulties is complex, particularly when children present inconsistent profiles characterised by strong ability, poor social skills, emotional immaturity and underachievement. It is important to note that children's abilities emerge at different ages and under different circumstances. Thus, identification must be an ongoing process throughout all key stages of children's development and take into consideration diverse aspects of their functioning.

A wide range of identification strategies, mainly qualitative, can be useful to identify behaviours associated with giftedness in young children. Teacher observations across different contexts, i.e. PE, performing arts, are likely to yield interesting results with regard to children's engagement in literacy activities and, most importantly, their approach, attitudes and dispositions, the strategies they use, the questions they ask and the extent to which they take initiative and engage in independent learning. Also, checklists to identify characteristics/behaviours that are associated with able students are a useful starting point when discussing pupils' profiles with their parents and other

practitioners. Checklists should be used with caution though, in that their validity may be questionable. Finally, gathering information from a range of sources, including parents, external agencies such as sports clubs, peers and the children themselves, is crucial.

Assessing language and literacy in EAL children requires you to focus on both the learner (e.g. child's proficiency in oral and written language) and the learning situation (e.g. family context, the value placed on child's first language, teaching methods and styles, liaison between parents and classroom staff). A review done by Cline and Shamsi (2000) found that there is very limited research in the area of assessing language and literacy in EAL children. Evaluating children's home or first language is problematic, and there are several reasons that may explain this. As I discussed in Chapter 2, a subgroup of EAL children, i.e. those from refugee/asylum seeking families, are likely to experience upheaval and, perhaps, social disadvantage. Their families are not reached easily and, thus, you and other classroom staff are less likely to access information about their prior learning experiences, the values their parents place on language learning, the language(s) they speak at home, the developmental history of the child and concerns with literacy in their first language. What also makes the process of collecting information about EAL children difficult is the lack of valid assessment devices for a wide range of languages, compounded by a number of other concerns with assessing English as discussed in Chapter 2.

Children with hearing difficulties are also likely to present language and communication difficulties putting a further obstacle to their learning. Hearing difficulties have an impact on children's functioning in the classroom and playground, which is not easily quantifiable, affecting their participation in classroom activities and discussions, interactions with peers and adults, and the ability to follow instructions and access the curriculum. Hearing impairment typically becomes evident during the early stages of children's development, around the second year of age where important linguistic developments occur. The initial signs of hearing difficulties that should raise the alarm include children having frequent ear infections, poor sound discrimination, incorrect pronunciation of certain letters and words and an overall restricted and immature language. Young children with hearing impairment tend to display certain behaviours in that they

- appear to lack concentration or switch off
- engage in daydreaming or become withdrawn to their own world
- look at their teachers very intensely and attempt to lip-read
- may display behavioural difficulties, e.g. frustration, temper tantrums
- present an inconsistent hearing depending on where they stand in the classroom and the noise in the external environment
- tend to speak unusually loud without realising it
- experience difficulties with processing sounds (phonological skills) and
- display difficulties following instructions and tend to follow what others do and then engage in a task (Frederickson and Cline, 2002).

### Language and communication

Communication encompasses many skills, namely linguistic skills (syntax and grammar) and knowledge of word meanings; social knowledge and symbolic skills manifested in

make-believe play and discussions of real and fictional situations; ability to decipher social cues, be aware of cultural norms and infer about others' feelings and thoughts (theory of mind); and use language to address emotions and thoughts. The ability to infer about others' thoughts and feelings (theory of mind) in particular is linked to communication in that children's capacity to take others' perspective is thought to be a prerequisite to understanding and using words such as 'think', 'believe' or 'remember' (Woolley, 1995). Specifically, by the age of four, children normally understand words such as 'know', 'pretend', 'understand', 'believe', and are able to engage in pretend play with three or more logically connected ideas. During the pre-school years, joint pretend play emerges where children understand the pretend actions and language used by play partners (Pershey, 2000). Pretend or symbolic play is a prerequisite for the development of good communication skills. Children with difficulties engaging in symbolic play do not sequence events and cannot take others in play, nor do they give intention to dolls or other toys they use, resulting in a restricted use of language (Westby, 1999).

Assessing young children's communication requires a qualitative approach to enable you to consider the context within which language is produced. This can be achieved by observing language in different natural contexts and recording and analysing the language samples produced (by applying discourse analysis). The development of children's language and communication begins within the family. Thus, through close liaison with children's families, you may obtain information about language development and ensure consistency regarding language intervention strategies.

Language samples produced during social interaction are also useful to evaluate children's social knowledge and communication skills. Specifically, you may look for evidence of language used for

- social purposes, such as greeting, requesting comfort, attempting to enter a group or initiate interaction;
- behavioural/emotional regulation primarily in terms of requesting an object, taking turns and resolving conflict instead of acting out;
- negotiation purposes in terms of taking turns to engage in an activity, or protesting when feeling that they have been treated unjustly;
- communicating across familiar and unfamiliar situations;
- different purposes with different conversational partners (e.g. adults, children);
- using emotion words to express their and others' feelings (positive and negative) – for example a child who is upset or withdrawn/shy may use language in a developmentally immature or inappropriate way;
- playing and interacting with peers in terms of understanding others' emotion (e.g. puppet gets upset because she did not get the toy she wanted).

It has been suggested that children as young as five are aware of language even if they do not reflect on it (Nicholas, 1991). This metalinguistic awareness is expressed in their ability to engage in storytelling and narratives, and generally talk about events that are not 'here and now' but 'there and then'. Hewitt and Duchan (1995) stated that assessing children's storytelling is an effective way of evaluating their ability to talk about the main character's feelings, thoughts and intent, and speak from the character's point of view to express how the character feels and thinks. Observing children's language use during storytelling and pretend play is helpful to assess their spontaneous

use of language. During storytelling, a range of communicative skills are displayed, including

- imaginative language to express fantasy and engage in pretend
- language to acquire knowledge through questioning, clarifying and expanding
- regulatory language to influence others and engage in problem solving and
- personal language in terms of descriptions about own feelings and thoughts (Pershey, 2000).

Although there is a limited professional agreement with regard to the areas of language that assessment should focus on in young children, phonics and communication skills are emphasised. Evaluation of communication skills in young children requires practitioners to consider children's social knowledge, symbolic play, perspective taking and the ability to use language for emotional/behavioural regulation. The main goal of language and communication assessment in young children is to inform the teaching of language as part of the Foundation Stage curriculum. With this in mind, assessing children's language skills should not be separated from evaluating their emotional and social development. It is not easy to untangle these areas of development and focus on one without considering the other. Consequently, the suggestions about assessing social-emotional development share common principles with those for assessing language and communication.

### Social and emotional development

The following guidelines have been adapted from Prizant's (1999) assessment framework that incorporates both communication and social-emotional aspects of young children's development. This framework succeeds in bringing together language and social-emotional skills, stressing the need for an integrated approach towards assessment and classroom practice. Nursery and reception teachers and other early years practitioners may ask children's parents questions about their children's social interaction, emotional expression and communicative competence to establish young children's language and social skills.

Social interaction and emotional expression with peers and adults are the cornerstones for good communication skills, emotional maturity and social adjustment. Through interactions with peers, children gain an understanding of the cultural and societal norms, develop a point of reference as to what appropriate behaviour is and learn how to express feelings and thoughts. Observations of children's peer interactions and discussions with family members are helpful to accumulate information to answer the following questions:

- Does the child typically prefer to be close to others (younger/older peers, siblings and adults)?
- Does the child respond to and initiate social interaction, for example through games, routines, greeting?
- Does the child's body language and facial expressions (e.g. gaze shifting from one person to the other; face-to-face gaze) suggest motivation/desire to interact with others?
- How often does the child use language for requests, greeting, etc.?
- Does the child establish eye contact with others or observe their activities?

- Does the child attempt to establish joint attention verbally or pre-verbally by commenting or requesting information, or through gestures?
- Is the child able to initiate and maintain conversational topics of interest?
- Does the child imitate actions, language or body language of others?
- Does the child forms emotional attachment with a nursery staff or other adult with whom he/she spends a reasonable period of time?
- Does the child use relationships with adults as a secure basis for comfort and emotional support?
- Does the child express a wide range of emotions through language, facial expressions or body language?
- Does the child share emotions with others?
- Does the child recognise and respond appropriately to the emotions of others?
- Does the child display or express concerns or actively attempt to comfort another child in distress through expression of empathy? (Prizant, 1999; paraphrased)

## Quantitative assessment: phonology, reading and writing

Thus far, I discussed qualitative approaches to assess young children's language, social and literacy development. In this section, I would like to present quantitative approaches to the assessment of pre-literacy (i.e. phonological skills) and literacy (reading and writing) by using standardised tests, in conjunction with qualitative assessment procedures, to provide information about children's learning needs. There are two main categories of tests available, norm-referenced and criterion-referenced. Norm-referenced tests provide information about individual children's performance in comparison with the performance on the same task of a representative group of children of the same age and gender in a particular geographical area. Criterion-referenced tests provide information about an individual child's performance compared to the goals set for this particular child by taking into consideration his/her needs. The majority of tests presented here are norm-referenced.

### Phonology tests

There are a number of useful, norm-referenced tests to explore children's phonological development.

A test titled 'Phonological Assessment Battery' was developed by Norah Frederickson, Uta Frith and Rea Reason in 1997 (Windsor: NFER-Nelson) to assess children's phonological skills. It is suitable for children aged six to fourteen, and contains six sub-tests focusing on different aspects of phonological development such as alliteration, naming speed, rhyme, spoonerisms, fluency and non-word reading.

Another test of phonological development that can be easily used is the Children's Test of Non-word Repetition developed by Gathercole and Baddeley in 1996. It contains a list of non-words (not real words) for children from as young as four to read. Difficulties in pronouncing correctly these words suggest phonological problems with regard to understanding and manipulating sounds and deciphering words. This is a useful test for early years settings and a good diagnostic tool for assessing young children's phonological processing and raise alarm regarding the possibility of dyslexia.

The Phonological Abilities Test (PAT) was also developed for young children aged five to seven, by The Psychological Corporation Ltd. It contains six sub-tests namely rhyme identification, rhyme production, word completion, phoneme identification, speech rate and letter knowledge.

### Reading tests

Reading tests normally focus on single-word recognition, i.e. deciphering/pronouncing words out of the context of a paragraph, and reading comprehension where children are asked to read a number of paragraphs and answer comprehension questions (e.g. factual questions, prediction questions and other inferential questions). The following tests are useful for assessing children's reading skills at a word, sentence and text level.

Graded Word Reading Test (Windsor: NFER-Nelson) is used to test children aged six to fourteen, and can be used with Y2 children who present dyslexia-associated difficulties to assess their word-recognition skills. Likewise, the Word Recognition and Phonics Skills (WRAPS), suitable for children aged five to eight for group or individual administration, focuses on assessing reading at a word level.

Reading comprehension at sentence and passage level can be assessed by the NFER Group Reading Test II. (Windsor: NFER-Nelson). This can be used for Y2 pupils and is administered in groups or individually. Children are asked to complete sentences by selecting words from a given list, involving knowledge of grammar and syntax and comprehension skills.

### Spelling tests

The Parallel Spelling Test was developed by Young (Sevenoaks: Hodder and Stoughton), and is suitable for ages between five and eleven. The target words are presented in the context of sentences to guide children to apply spelling rules and patterns correctly.

These reading- and spelling-standardised tests are fairly easy to use, with their results providing useful information about young children's phonological development, spelling and reading at a word, sentence and text level. It is important that reception and nursery staff are supported by the Special Educational Needs Co-ordinator (SENCO) or other professionals to administer and interpret these tests, and use the results constructively to inform their teaching.

### Dyslexia screening tests

Early years staff are also in the position to obtain initial information regarding the possibility of dyslexia by administering dyslexia screening tests. There are several tests developed for this purpose; however, I would like to focus on two tests in particular that have been found to have a good predictive validity.

The first test is the Bangor Dyslexia Test developed by Miles in 1989. This test can be used with children aged seven or older and explores characteristics and behaviours that are associated with dyslexia such as left–right confusion and difficulty with sequencing (e.g. months of the year, days of the week, times tables).

The second test is the Dyslexia Early Screening Test – 2nd edition (DEST-II) developed for four- to six-year olds. It provides information about areas found to be associated with dyslexia, such as rapid naming (information processing), phonological discrimination, bead threading (fine motor skills), postural stability (gross motor skills), rhyme detection (phonological awareness), digit span (short-term memory and sequencing skills), recognition of letters and numbers, sound order and copying shapes. DEST-II has been developed by Fawcett and Nicolson (1999) and is published by the Psychological Corporation Ltd.

I would like to conclude this chapter by stressing the need to take both a qualitative and a quantitative approach to obtaining information about children's learning and development. Standardised test scores, observations across different settings (e.g. classroom, playground), discussions with parents and other professionals are useful sources of information about young children's learning and development. Most importantly, however, you, as a practitioner, should ascertain the views and the wishes of the children themselves and involve them in the assessment process, particularly children who are able to express their views about learning. Both the Code of Practice and the Article 12 of the United Nations Convention on the Rights of the Child emphasise children's rights to express their thoughts and feelings for situations that primarily concern them. It is important to note, however, that with very young children and children with language and communication difficulties, expressing their views may not be realistically possible, requiring assistance from adults.

## Summary

There has been an ongoing debate regarding the approaches taken for identifying and diagnosing young children's needs, and the developmental appropriateness of early years assessment devices and procedures. Also, the validity of the information obtained and its usefulness to inform classroom practice has been critiqued extensively. Current SEN legislation and policy stress the need for taking an interactional approach towards evaluation in terms of assessing both the learner and the learning situation qualitatively and quantitatively. As an early year practitioner, you are well placed to gather rich information about children's language, social and literacy development. You need, however, to be aware of the grey area within which you operate when assessing young children whose development varies greatly. Working closely with parents is likely to stimulate good practice given that children's learning experiences are shaped within their families, allowing you to gain an understanding of the complex interaction between children's experiences and school's expectations and culture of learning. This is particularly important for EAL children whose needs are diverse, and for gifted children whose profiles of strengths and needs are seen as being paradoxical, posing serious challenges to both parents and educators.

Chapter 5

# Effectiveness in early years teaching and learning

## Introduction

Effective teaching and learning has been debated extensively, especially within the context of school improvement. Raising standards in literacy and numeracy in a quantifiable and measurable way lies in the heart of every political agenda. Among educators, there is a strong interest in taking an evidence-based approach to teaching and learning in terms of collecting and interpreting information about children's performance and using the evidence generated to guide classroom practice. Over the last years, however, the usefulness and relevance of educational research with regard to helping teachers ensure that all children learn successfully, especially those with literacy difficulties, has been critiqued extensively (Hargreaves, 1996). Although there have been many attempts to synthesise research on literacy and its implications for classroom instruction, the greatest concern with applying educational research to inform classroom practice is the sheer amount of the research itself, as well as making judgements about what is relevant and what is not.

With this in mind, the Early Years Curriculum Group (1989) has taken an evidence-based approach towards identifying key strategies that underlie effective teaching and learning in early years education. These strategies include drawing links between young children's education and their own experiences and prior knowledge, considering children's social experiences and interaction, encouraging children's participation and providing opportunities for them to become independent learners. All these can be achieved by supporting children to engage in 'active learning', 'interactive learning', 'decision-making', 'reflecting' and 'interpreting' (Early Years Curriculum Group, 1989: 14, 15).

## Early years teaching and learning: making a good start

The term literacy has become quite prominent in a growing knowledge society where individuals are expected to engage in life-long learning. The definition for literacy is constantly expanding to include, in addition to reading and writing, speaking and listening skills and knowledge of ICT.

Wray and Shilvock provided a detailed definition of literacy as

the ability to read and use written information, and to write appropriately for a range of purposes. It also involves the integration of speaking, listening and critical thinking with reading and writing, and includes the knowledge that enables a speaker, writer or reader to recognise and use language appropriate to different social situations.

(2003: 8)

This definition emphasises the importance of language, particularly the communicative function of language. It suggests a departure from narrow understandings of literacy, i.e. reading and writing skills, to embrace areas such as language, social knowledge, emotional literacy and knowledge of ICT. In a knowledge economy, good quality education is expected to go beyond mere acquisition of content knowledge, to support children's understanding of the world, social interactions, communicative competence, emotional maturity, resilience, resourcefulness and adaptability. This is a tall order for any educational system to achieve, especially when catering for children with a wide range of SEN, as well as children from families experiencing social and economic disadvantage and reduced opportunities.

In previous chapters, I stressed the need for taking an integrated approach to meeting the needs of young children with dyslexia by focusing on their linguistic, social-emotional and educational development. Taking an integrated approach to children's development is also reflected in current understandings of literacy, as well as in the evolution of the early years curriculum whose focus has expanded over the years to include language, social skills, play and emotional development.

## The making of early years curriculum

In England, considerable changes have been taking place regarding the development of the curriculum for children under five. In 1996, specific learning goals for four- and five-year olds were introduced in the form of Desirable Outcomes for Children's Learning focusing on six areas of learning, including language and literacy (SCAA, 1996). Although this framework was not supposed to be overly prescribed, it set the structure for early years education by drawing links to the National Curriculum in primary schools. Many of the learning outcomes described in the Desirable Outcomes for Children's Learning document refer to formal notions of literacy such as recognising the letters of the alphabet and writing their name with appropriate use of upper and lower case letters, with play and activity-orientated learning barely being mentioned.

In 1999, the revised Early Learning Goals were introduced including 19 goals for literacy and language to be achieved by the end of the Foundation Stage (QCA, 1999). The introduction of the Foundation Stage Curriculum for children aged three to five set the framework for monitoring and assessing young children's learning within the context of professional accountability and standards. Many professionals in the field of early childhood felt that, although the revised guidance includes play as an important aspect of learning, the focus of the curriculum is on 'what' and not on 'how' children learn (Carvel, 1999; Miller, 2000).

There were concerns raised with regard to the 'content-driven' early years pedagogy, focusing on instructional strategies with limited engagement in play and activity-orientated learning (Anning and Edwards, 1999). Many changes have been put forward as a response to these concerns, stressing the importance of communication skills, social interactions, play and learning experiences for young children's development (QCA, 2000). The Curriculum Guidance for the Foundation Stage (QCA, 2000) was introduced to ensure that reception children have their own curriculum, and assist early years practitioners in implementing and planning towards the Early Learning Goals (QCA, 1999), replacing the Desirable Outcomes for Children's Learning. Moreover, the introduction of the FSP for five-year olds, in which literacy is one of the areas to be assessed, is a new development regarding assessment, identification and early years provision.

Along with the National Curriculum, the National Literacy Strategy (NLS) has dominated literacy teaching in the early years. It has been seen as one option among others in raising standards in literacy. A number of policy options emerging from the implementation of the NLS are:

- To alter the curriculum, methods, timing and intensity of early years education.
- To adjust teaching to meet the needs of children who are socially disadvantaged.
- To intervene systematically with children who had fallen behind in literacy during the first year of teaching by providing an intense catch-up programme (e.g. Reading Recovery). And
- To provide remedial teaching in small groups or 1:1 in the mainstream. (DfEE, 1998).

Piotrowski and Reason (2000) compared the approaches used to teaching pupils with dyslexia to those introduced by the NLS. It was found that the issue of reciprocal assessment and teaching, i.e. use of assessment to inform teaching, was prominent in both programmes. The NLS itself did not provide enough guidance, though, on ways of establishing what children have learned and how to follow specific strategies to ensure that their learning is continuous. Thus, there is a need for clarity and specification regarding the materials used and the teaching strategies employed. Reason (2001) also identified some problems with regard to applying the NLS framework to support children with dyslexia-associated difficulties. Specifically, in Y1 (five–six-year olds), the learning targets set are considered to be ambitious and thus some children are likely to display learning difficulties due to the structure and the degree of difficulty of the materials. Consequently, children with dyslexia can be doubly disadvantaged in reaching the leaning standards set by the NLS framework.

## Early years practitioners: What does it take to become effective?

Traditionally, educators and other child professionals have been working within the context of the 'deficiency model' where children are viewed as having deficits and child professionals are expected to provide remedial services. In the 1980s, the deficiency model expanded to also include notions of deficit within the communities. Although this was seen as a progress in that deficit is not necessarily located within the individual child but within the wider social, cultural and economic context, the deficit model reduces diversity into difficulties. A 'difficulties' approach has shaped professional roles and responsibilities to a great extent, and moving away from this would require early years staff to engage in innovative thinking and challenge old models of SEN provision.

In the early 1990s, Pascal pointed out the challenges that reception staff experience with the implementation of the National Curriculum, owing to limited training and lack of support to cater for young children's learning and social and emotional development (1990). For early years staff, catering for young children with SEN is doubly challenging, in that they are expected to apply strategies and approaches to teaching, without having sufficient knowledge regarding their effectiveness.

In a study by Moyles *et al.* (2002), effectiveness was understood in terms of achieving high standards in literacy and numeracy, as well as supporting children develop social skills for negotiation, conflict resolution, perspective taking, empathy and competency in using language for learning and as a social tool. Moreover, in a study by Siraj-Blatchford *et al.* (2002), the characteristics and competencies of effective early years practitioners were summarised in terms of setting appropriate challenges, celebrating success, interacting with children verbally and engaging in activity-based learning through the use of play and drama.

Although there is a growing recognition of the importance of activity-based learning, early years practitioners find it particularly difficult to implement. Bennett *et al.* (1997) delineated the barriers that early years practitioners experience in using play for teaching and learning. Specifically, factors that are likely to hinder play include parental expectations, rigid curriculum guidelines and school timetables and resources. Also, the increasing emphasis on raising standards and performance indicators is likely to restrict play as a valid teaching and learning method in that its learning outcomes are not directly measurable and quantifiable.

Early years professionals are expected to take reasonable steps to ensure that children's learning and social-emotional needs are met by providing experiences that benefit all young children, and particularly those with learning difficulties. Using appropriate language in the classroom and the playground and encouraging pupils' diverse learning styles and cultural/social values are the cornerstones of the good quality of early years education and care. Catering for young children requires knowledge of child development issues and an awareness of family/community influences and practices. It also requires practitioners to develop an understanding of issues about social equity and equal opportunities with regard to children accessing services and resources, and become receptive to the values and beliefs that young children bring in early years classrooms.

Moreover, in planning activities that promote younger children's development and learning, early years practitioners should consider a number of issues regarding their own personal and professional development. Early years staff, especially those who work closely with families experiencing social and economic disadvantage, need to rethink their expectations and attitudes and become aware of the ways these are communicated to children and their families. Principles of equal opportunities, confidentiality and anti-stereotypical thinking should permeate early years educators' daily practice. Children learn from the quality of relationships among staff and between staff and pupils, their parents and the community. As Booth and his colleagues (2000) argue, early years professionals working with young children and their parents from ethnically and socially diverse communities should consider

- their own biases towards minority groups;
- the potential impact of social exclusion from the dominant culture on families and young children;
- the meaning of group identity and how this affects child rearing practices; and
- stereotypical views about children's diverse cultural and social backgrounds, and how they affect parent–professional interactions and parental involvement.

In this context, working with young children as either a newly qualified teacher, a nursery nurse or a learning support assistant is likely to bring personal and professional changes. At a personal level, it makes you re-examine your beliefs and ideas about learning and child development, test your limitations and open up to the scrutiny from your peers and think about your own values. With regard to the last point, Orlik (2004) argues that new teachers should examine the values that underlie their professional practice in the light of current legislative and policy frameworks, and in the context of the specific early years setting within which they operate. This is particularly important in that values underlie many aspects of schools' functioning including the curriculum (both explicit and implicit), teaching approaches (didactic or child-centred), ethos, partnerships with families and communities and staff collaboration.

At a professional level, a major challenge you are likely to face is combining content knowledge and teaching approaches with an understanding of children's emotional, social and linguistic functioning to meet their diverse needs. Teaching a set of skills is not enough, nor is it desirable. Shulman referred to the pedagogic content knowledge which is an amalgam between content and pedagogy or, in other words, a blending of curriculum, instructional methods, teacher–pupil interactions, pupils' abilities and teachers' views (Shulman, 1987).

## Professional development: peer coaching

The changing roles of early years practitioners have prompted the implementation of professional development strategies to improve the quality of their practice. Professional development is a critical aspect of school improvement initiatives in early years education nationally and internationally. Professional development programmes in the USA have introduced peer coaching, among other strategies, for teachers and classroom staff (National Commission on Teaching and America's Future, 1996; National Staff Development Council, 2001). In the article 'The Evolution of Peer Coaching', Showers and Joyce (1996) approached professional coaching from a historical perspective. They argued that 'teachers who had a coaching relationship, that is, who shared aspects of teaching, planned together and pooled their experiences, practised new skills and strategies more frequently and applied them more appropriately' than did their colleagues who worked alone to expand their repertoires (1996: 14). Peer coaching typically involves collaborative planning, observation and feedback, rather than a formal evaluation or review of teachers' work.

There are many different types of coaching with the most effective being the so-called 'collegial coaching', which seeks to improve existing teacher practices by refining techniques, developing collegiality, increasing professional dialogue and assisting teachers to reflect on their teaching (Becker, 1996). Findings from research on induction programmes show that newly qualified teachers benefit more from formal peer coaching than informal interactions with their colleagues (Klug and Salzman, 1991). Moreover, peer-coaching programmes have been found to encourage professional growth, recognition, experience-enhancing roles and collegiality for all practitioners involved, i.e. beginning teachers and more experienced ones. Specifically, effective peer-coaching programmes have important implications for

- promoting the ethos and culture of early years settings
- improving instructional capacity through mentoring and classroom guidance
- supporting collaboration among staff and
- encouraging practitioners to draw links between policy and practice (Killion, 1990).

There is controversy as to whether peer coaching should be used for evaluating teachers and other classroom staff during a peer review process. For early years practitioners in particular, whose roles have undergone rapid transformations lately, peer coaching should remain distinct from evaluation and used as a system of collegial support. Peer coaching, as a professional development strategy, shares many similarities with inter-professional collaboration, both aiming at establishing a culture that is conducive to

- the development of trust relationships among practitioners
- supporting practitioners at personal, organisational and financial/resource level
- acknowledging and recognising staff professional development
- clarifying expectations and roles for staff, pupils and parents and
- providing constructive feedback, time commitment and financial assistance (Becker, 1996)

## Early years teaching for dyslexia: instructional strategies

The Curriculum Guidance for the Foundation Stage addresses the skills, understandings and concepts that children need to develop by the end of the Foundation Stage to enable them to acquire formal literacy (reading and writing) successfully. These include:

- Link sounds to letters, naming and sounding the letters of the alphabet.
- Use their phonic knowledge to write simple regular words and make attempts at sounding more complex words.
- Re-tell narratives in the correct sequence, drawing on language patterns found in stories.
- Read a range of familiar and common words and simple sentences independently.
- Show an understanding of the elements of a story, such as the main character, sequence of events, and openings and how information can be found in non-fiction texts to answer questions about where, who, why and how.
- Attempt writing for different purposes, using features of different forms such as lists, stories and instructions.
- Write their own name and other things such as labels and captions, and begin to form simple sentences, sometimes using punctuation.
- Use a pencil and hold it effectively to form recognisable letters (DfEE/QCA, 2000: 60, 62, 64, 66).

To assist young children with dyslexia in developing these understandings and skills, classroom instruction should be both *interactive* and *reactive*. Interactive instruction emphasises the interaction between the pupils' profiles, the evidence obtained regarding their needs through assessment, interviews with family members and observations, the ways in which evidence is viewed, treated and understood and the demands of the learning activities. The main assumption of interactive instruction is that all these elements are interconnected, enabling early years staff to draw clear links between children's strengths/weaknesses and provision.

A reactive instruction considers young children holistically, in an attempt to piece together their profile of needs and capabilities in the context of early years provision. During reactive instruction, the objectives and learning outcomes are re-adjusted to accommodate pupils' needs, suggesting flexibility in supporting children educationally and socially. Reactive teaching encourages calibration and adjustment of the learning goals, objectives and outcomes to meet children's diverse needs (see differentiation in Chapter 1). Thus, reactive classroom instruction requires devising and implementing specific criteria to document pupils' progress and delineate areas for further improvement.

Interactive and reactive classroom strategies can be used for formal literacy and the development of language and social-emotional skills. Regarding formal literacy, these strategies can be implemented across subject areas (i.e. reading, writing, arithmetic) and within the NLS. The NLS provides the structure for raising literacy standards by recognising that certain factors such as socio-economic deprivation, SEN and limited access to resources have an adverse impact on children's academic achievement. The NLS framework has three strands:

1   Word level: focusing on spelling, vocabulary and phonics
2   Sentence level: focusing on grammar and punctuation and
3   Text level: focusing on comprehension and composition.

In literacy, the NLS strands are reflected in the knowledge of the alphabetic system (symbols and sounds); phonemic awareness instruction to support word decoding and fluent reading; and comprehension of text (at a word, sentence and text level). The National Association for Special Educational Needs (NASEN) has published a useful guide on identifying reading difficulties at a word and sentence level. At the word level, poor phonological difficulties are likely to hinder children's understanding about how sounds and letters relate to each other, resulting in difficulties deciphering unknown words. At the sentence level, children may have difficulties integrating the information they get and extract meaning due to grammatical and syntactical difficulties and their restricted knowledge of semantics (word meaning). Finally, comprehension difficulties, at text level, can be evident even when children recognise individual words and read fluently.

During reading in particular, pupils need to apply phonetic rules accurately and consistently to decipher words (word level); if not, their chances of pronouncing words correctly are limited. At the sentence level, when vocabulary is unknown and the sentences are complex grammatically and syntactically, children with language difficulties and/or dyslexia are less equipped to make connections between words, draw links with what they already know and extract meaning. Clearly, language is implicated in reading at both word and sentence level, affecting reading comprehension considerably (Hartas, 2005).

We know from research on the effectiveness of reading programmes that certain types of pre-school interventions for reading work better than others. Specifically, the reading strategies for building phonology and reading comprehension have brought positive results, especially with young children. It is crucial to ensure that young children with dyslexia benefit from reading instructions at a word, sentence and text level given that reading skills cut across the curriculum, enabling them to make a good start with their education.

## Reading at word level: building phonology

Over the last decades there has been an accumulation of research on the role that phonological skills play in children's reading and writing (e.g. Stringer and Stanovich,

2000; Snowling, 1995). The most widely accepted explanation for reading difficulties in young children has been difficulties processing the phonological features of language in terms of analysing and synthesising sounds and linking them to letters. Phonological difficulties normally become apparent at the early stages of schooling, e.g. nursery and reception, and are currently viewed as the core problem underlying reading difficulties, including dyslexia. Research on the effectiveness of phonological training programmes suggests that the group of children who benefit the most are pre-school children in terms of improving skills such as phoneme segmentation, blending and deletion to enable them manipulate the sounds that comprise words (Nicolson, 1999).

As children develop basic reading skills they go through several stages, including the alphabetic stage where they begin to link letters (graphemes) to their corresponding sounds (phonemes). The awareness of the links between letters and sounds enables pupils to recognise the initial sounds of unfamiliar words and sound them out. For children with dyslexia, supporting reading at word level is important in that their phonological knowledge with regard to making links between letters and sounds is restricted, impacting on word decoding and word recognition significantly.

The term phonological skills is frequently used when discussing children's development of basic reading and spelling skills. But what does it really mean? As I mentioned in Chapter 1, phonology is an aspect of language, referring to the system of sounds. Young children show phonological awareness by recognising syllables (e.g. clap once for each syllable in a word), being increasingly able to divide syllables into onset and rime, identify words that rhyme (e.g. bat/hat), segmenting the words into all their sounds and deleting or changing the position of certain sounds.

In the literature of reading, phonological development is discussed along phonological awareness, phonological sensitivity and phonological processing. Phonological awareness involves recognition of sounds and sound patterns in spoken language. Oakhill and Garnham (1989) described phonological awareness as the ability to detect, distinguish and manipulate not just the phonemes (i.e. smallest meaningful units of sound in a language) but also onset rimes and syllables. It is important to draw a distinction between phonemes and syllables in that phonological awareness is thought to proceed from an awareness of syllables to an awareness of phonemes.

Phonological sensitivity refers to the recognition of certain phonological aspects of language such as rhyme and alliteration. There is a strong connection between knowledge of nursery rhymes in children at the age of three and their development of phonological sensitivity and basic reading during the pre-school years (Stanovich, 1988). Phonological processing refers to making use of the sounds of spoken language during the decoding of written language (Adams, 1990). Children begin to decode unfamiliar words by 'translating' the letters to sounds, moving from a visual form to an auditory one.

For the majority of children, phonological development follows a relatively predictable path in terms of acquiring phonological skills through nursery rhymes and songs and conversations with peers and parents. However, for many children with dyslexia, the acquisition of phonological skills is a long and laborious process, starting with an awareness of syllables and building up to understanding and manipulating individual sounds and translating them to letters. There are two levels of difficulty embedded in developing phonological skills. The first level is poor rhyme detection and auditory discrimination, in that it is easier for children to detect large sound units (e.g. rhyme, syllables) than small ones (e.g. phoneme). The second level of difficulty refers to the awareness of phonemes, and the attainment of this level depends on developing an alphabetic understanding, i.e. knowledge of the letter/sound correspondences, manifested during phoneme synthesis and phoneme analysis tasks.

Cooke (2002) has compiled a list of behaviours and skills that are associated with the development of phonological skills. This list is useful to help you and other classroom staff identify pupils who are suspected to have phonological difficulties. Specifically, you may check whether a pupil:

- can separate individual words in the flow of speech
- is aware of the sounds that comprise single words
- can identify words that rhyme
- knows how to blend the sounds of a word
- makes correspondences between single sounds and letters
- differentiates between vowels and consonants
- builds words consisting of consonants and vowels
- deciphers words that he/she has not seen before and
- separates and blends sounds automatically during reading.

There are many tasks to support phonological awareness in children with dyslexia. One characteristic of these tasks is that words are presented by utilising different modalities, such as verbal, visual and kinaesthetic. Some of these tasks involve

- auditory discrimination;
- manipulation of sounds in terms of blending, segmentation, deletion, isolation, counting and substitution of phonemes/sounds; and
- rhyming, tapping, etc.

Classroom strategies focusing on phonological development and word recognition take a multi-sensory approach to literacy. These involve a series of steps stressing the simultaneous use of visual, auditory and tactile modalities. For example, children with dyslexia are encouraged to look at a word, pronounce it and then incorporate it into a sentence. They may also be asked to trace the word in the air and to spell it orally. Young children with dyslexia may benefit from phonologically based instructions to develop basic reading skills. Reading strategies at word level include:

- an intensive, structured, multi-sensory approach to reading;
- a preview of all reading materials to establish background knowledge prior to reading;
- the use of prefixes and suffixes to illustrate changes in meaning and enhance vocabulary development, for Y1 and Y2 pupils in particular;
- sound blending skills and the presentation of new words linguistically by focusing on root words, prefixes and suffixes;
- contextual decoding including picture cues or reminding pupils of the main idea, simultaneously drawing their attention to initial letters to narrow down the word choices; and
- practice with sight word vocabulary by placing new words children encounter on cards and reviewing them daily for proficiency.

To support children's phonological development, it is important to note that phonological training is not an end in itself; rather, it gives children the initial tools they need to start decoding and recognising words. As children move towards the orthographic stage, they are able to recognise clusters of letters, such as suffixes and prefixes and familiar patterns, and analyse words into orthographic units.


## Reading at sentence and text level: making meaning

When reading for meaning making, children do not always read the text word by word. Some children may use pictures and other contextual cues to construct their own text. With young children, engaging in pretend reading is fun and makes a good use of their imagination. Pretend reading is also less threatening in terms of engaging young children with dyslexia in reading, in that they are encouraged to discuss their own version of the text without being constrained by their limited recognition of words. In your classroom, you can choose a book relevant to pupils' interests and introduce it by talking about the illustration of its cover and the pictures inside. Next, you may ask children to predict what the book is about by linking it with other books they know. Finally, you may go through the book pages and talk about its content by pointing to pictures.

It is essential to plan pretend reading activities so you know where to stop to invite questions or initiate a conversation by encouraging children's comments. Questions can range from simple factual ones, such as 'What is this picture at the book cover?', to more experiential questions, such as 'How does the main character feel?', to help children recognise the meaning of individual words. At the end of pretend reading, you may stimulate discussions by drawing links between what the children know and the new information provided. This is the 'extended text' phase, thought to facilitate reading comprehension and language (Harker, 1988; Raphael and McMahon, 1994).

Harker argues that discussions surrounding text expand the boundaries of reading by focusing on the text and the conversation that is socially constructed as children interact with one another and the text, resulting in extending the text (1988). Discussions during reading also encourage a dynamic approach towards meaning making by taking others' point of view and interpreting their thoughts, clarifying expectations and negotiating the purpose of reading and, ultimately, monitoring their own understanding. In the USA, the Book Club programme, for example, scaffolds children's reading comprehension through conversations by suggesting ways of talking about the text (Raphael and McMahon, 1994). This programme supports reading by integrating language and literacy goals within the context of collaborative classroom interactions (i.e. whole-class discussions, pupil-led group discussions).

Buddy reading is another good reading strategy, particularly for Y1 or Y2 pupils who may have already acquired some basic reading skills. Buddy reading is normally done by pairing up children, giving them a book of their choice and asking them to read it to their reading partner by taking turns reading books or different pages of the same book. It is a good strategy to engage pupils with reading difficulties or dyslexia in that their reading partner does not have to be at the same reading level. For example, you may pair a good reader with one who experiences reading difficulties or pair a less able reader with younger children to boost poor readers' self-confidence. You may also assume the role of the 'buddy' yourself to engage children with dyslexia and low self-confidence in reading by inviting them to say something about what you have read and, through this dialogue, stimulate their listening skills and expressive language. You may also expand their comprehension by encouraging children to make predictions about what is going to happen next and share their experiences related to the ideas derived from text.

Another way of engaging poor, Y1 and Y2 readers without putting them under pressure is through small interactive groups. These groups are organised and run by the children themselves who have read the same book and would like to share it with others. This is an interesting reading strategy that can be implemented during peer-mediated activities in particular (see Chapter 3 for a detailed discussion on peer mediation). Initially, you need to be present to help children run the group by modelling questions, elaborating on themes and turn-taking. Specifically, children should be encouraged to ask themselves questions such as:

- What do I remember from this book?
- How did I feel when I read about this character?
- What is my favourite part?
- What do I feel about the ideas in this book?
- What did the book make me think of?
- What questions would have I asked if the author were here?

These reading strategies targeting phonological skills and comprehension can be embedded in the NLS. The following is an example of reading instruction delivered within the structure of the Literacy Hour, illustrating the instructional approaches taken at the word, sentence and text level.

*Part one*: Whole class work at a text level with an emphasis on reading comprehension through the reading of a shared text (approximately 15 minutes).

*Part two*: Whole class work at word or sentence level in terms of teaching phonics, grammar and syntax, vocabulary and spelling (approximately 15 minutes).

*Part three*: Group or independent work with you or other classroom staff working with one ability group at a time, focusing on reading and writing at word or sentence level. During this time, the pupils not in the group working with the teacher work independently (approximately 20 minutes).

*Part four*: Whole class work in the form of a plenary session which aims at providing an overview of the work covered, consolidating new knowledge and giving the opportunity to both teacher and pupils to reflect on the lesson (approximately 10 minutes) (Bills and Brooks, 2004).

## EAL young pupils: literacy and language

As I discussed in Chapter 2, the number of multi-/bi-lingual children in British classrooms is on the rise. EAL children present many challenges to educators in that language development and literacy are interlinked and, thus, limited proficiency in language impacts on literacy and numeracy (Parke and Drury, 2001). This is particularly true for pupils who display dyslexia or literacy difficulties in their first language. Pang and Kamil (2004) referred to four models to explore the interaction between EAL and literacy development, each model reflecting different understandings of the links between language literacy and the instructional strategies put in place.

The first model stresses the importance of reaching oral proficiency in English or other additional language(s) before developing literacy in this language. The understanding is that through the development of listening and speaking, children will be able to read and write. This approach to reading development is consistent with the view that 'students should learn to listen, understand, and speak English in a natural way before they learn to read and write it' (Lapp and Flood, 1986: 320). Developing reading through language is seen as a matter of natural progression in children's development given that speaking precedes reading. This approach is also favoured in many classrooms where there is an emphasis on listening and speaking with a limited focus on reading. Developing oral proficiency is crucial, especially for young EAL children who may not be literate in their first language due to minimum exposure to print.

The second model refers to the development of reading and writing in children's first language while, simultaneously, they learn English. The expectation is that knowledge in literacy will transfer from the first language to the additional one, taking advantage of children's knowledge of their first language to develop educationally, and ensuring that they will not lag behind their peers. The idea that knowledge transfers across learning contexts has been critiqued extensively. As a practitioner, you may question whether knowledge transfers in children with dyslexia in particular.

The third model suggests a two-way interaction between children's first and additional language with an emphasis on maintaining the first language while literacy is developed through the additional language. Cazabon, Nicoladis and Lambert refer to this type of education as 'additive bi-lingualism' (1998, as cited in Pang and Kamil, 2004). There is evidence to suggest that additive bilingualism 'leads to better academic achievement because it gives due recognition to children's native language and culture, and in so doing, strengthens their self-concept and sense of achievement' (Pang and Kamil, 2004: 16). This is particularly important for those EAL children who have experienced social disadvantage and upheaval due to their refugee and/or asylum-seeking status.

The final, fourth model focuses exclusively on developing literacy through the medium of the additional language while it utilises the knowledge of other languages to reinforce reading and writing. The majority of the reading strategies discussed in this chapter rely on developing language skills. This is consistent with the findings from a study by Ramirez (1991), showing that using the first language to support reading does not impede the acquisition of English, and the guidance offered in the early years curriculum.

The Curriculum Guidance for the Foundation Stage (DfEE/QCA) recommends that young children with EAL should be offered opportunities and encouragement to participate in activities to support oral and written proficiency in English. Specifically, teachers and other classroom staff should

- take into account children's experiences and prior learning with regard to the language(s) spoken at home and the immediate community by giving them opportunities to use the home language(s) at school, so their developing use of English and other languages support one another;
- provide a wide range of opportunities for children to engage in speaking and listening activities in English with peers and adults;
- ensure that children's home language(s) are recognised and valued at school;
- provide bilingual support, particularly with vocabulary and language comprehension;
- provide exposure to writing in both English and home language(s); and
- provide opportunities for children to hear both English and home languages, for example, through the use of audio and video materials (2000: 19).

Clearly, language is implicated during reading at the word level (phonology), sentence level (grammar, syntax) and text level (meaning making through discussion and self-questioning). Young EAL children's reading and writing development can be severely compromised if they are not given the opportunity to develop speaking and listening skills in English and take into account their prior learning and linguistic experiences. As I discussed in Chapter 2, liaising with EAL children's families and valuing their culture and language are important for supporting these children to 'tune in' to the classroom and use their knowledge of different languages to learn English and access the curriculum.

## Summary

Effective teaching and learning takes a new meaning in a knowledge society where definitions of literacy constantly expand to include social-emotional literacy, the capacity to use language for thinking and as a social tool and knowledge of ICT. To ensure that learning is continuous, especially for children with dyslexia, early years staff face many challenges and paradoxes in terms of supporting children's diverse needs within the early years curriculum. In this context, one might consider the qualities and attributes required for early years staff to become effective and reflective practitioners. Clearly, as an early years educator, it takes more than acquiring content knowledge and applying classroom instructional strategies, including the ability to re-think your own values and expectations and communicate them to children and their families constructively. Finally, classroom strategies to support reading in children with dyslexia are presented by relying on language as the medium for learning.

# Chapter 6

# Information and communication technology

## Introduction

The development of information and communication technology (ICT) holds immense possibilities for young children with dyslexia and their teachers (Florian, 2004). Over the last decades information technology has been used to facilitate teaching and learning at a classroom and whole-school level. Currently, the increasing emphasis on educating children with SEN in the mainstream has reinforced the use of ICT as an effective way of modifying teaching and removing barriers to learning. Early ICT exposure in children is crucial to enable them to access the curriculum and facilitate their learning as they move to primary and secondary education.

Estelle Morris, the former Secretary of State for Education, stated that:

> I firmly believe that, when used in the right circumstances, ICT has huge potential to engage pupils in ways that will help them to realise their individual talents. It offers teachers new opportunities to develop their professional skills, whether in the classroom or in the virtual classroom.
>
> (DfES, 2002: 1)

This chapter discusses the use of ICT in teaching young children with dyslexia by making references to the statutory requirements to use ICT, and explores practical ways of using ICT in early years classrooms. It also presents strategies and methods in which computers and ICT can help young children with dyslexia and their teachers, providing many practical examples. The themes in this chapter are geared towards early years, focusing on supporting literacy and numeracy in children with dyslexia via the use of appropriate softwares; learning how to use softwares such as dictionaries and multimedia encyclopaedias; and accessing communication networks, email, games and the world wide web.

This chapter is organised into two sections. The first section discusses the use of ICT by early years teachers and practitioners to access resources and materials and interact with other colleagues to support their teaching. The second section focuses on specific classroom strategies that incorporate ICT to teach young children with dyslexia. To this end, I present research findings regarding the hindering and facilitative factors in teachers using ICT, and make suggestions about placing ICT in the existing curricular structures to make it relevant to the subject matter and supportive of inclusive learning. Finally, I address issues regarding the suitability and developmental appropriateness of using ICT with young children and provide guidelines for choosing programmes that are appropriate for young children.

## ICT: a tool for inclusion and responsive pedagogy

Among educators, there are high expectations that ICT is capable of facilitating a more equitable and democratic treatment of children with diverse needs, such as SEN, having the potential to support inclusion and remove obstacles to learning. There has also been a considerable debate as to whether and how this might be achieved (Florian, 2004). Despite the good welcome to ICT, research evidence suggests that, in many classrooms, ICT is used in a haphazard way without any obvious benefits to learning (Woodward and Rieth, 1997). On the contrary, some educators argue that ICT is liberating for children with severe physical disabilities (e.g. poor motor co-ordination) and speech and communication difficulties, in that it enables them to engage in tasks that would not be able to do otherwise (Florian, 2004).

ICT is also seen by many as a tool that facilitates inclusion (e.g. Reed and McNergney, 2000). However, thinking about the use of ICT as the cornerstone of inclusive learning may be an exaggeration in that, in the majority of classrooms, computers are used on an individual basis. An individual approach to using ICT questions whether working with computers to consolidate skills through drill and repetition constitutes inclusive learning. In this context, inclusion takes a new meaning by referring to a virtual interconnectivity whereby children communicate with each other in the cyberspace.

For early years, ICT has the potential to support emerging literacy and, hopefully, enable children transfer newly acquired skills from the virtual environment to the classroom and beyond. Research has shown that certain learners' characteristics such as ability and age have an effect on the effectiveness of ICT use for learning (Lou *et al.*, 2001). Although, evidence regarding the effectiveness and pedagogical appropriateness of using ICT in early years is limited, a couple of studies have found that proper use of ICT supports effective classroom practice. A study by Brooker and Siraj-Blatchford (2002) showed that children benefit from ICT in developing language and communication skills and learning. Specifically, nursery and reception children were observed to interact with each other while they were working with a computer, allowing them to practice language and communication skills, positive attitudes towards collaboration and social skills. In another study on ICT effectiveness, Riley found that the type of software used is a determining factor for successful ICT use, pointing out that software programmes that avoid 'single-answer, drill-and-skill based interaction offer more opportunities for collaboration and positive interactions' (2003: xxvi). Specifically, she mentioned two software programmes, namely Henry's Party (Marshal Media, 1995) and Tizzy's Toybox (Sherston Software, 1997), being effective in promoting social interactions and pro-social behaviour in children. Another important factor identified in Riley's study is the importance of practitioners' input in terms of knowing when to intervene and when to allow children engage in ICT-based tasks independently.

Moreover, when discussing issues regarding the developmental appropriateness of ICT and its capacity to remove obstacles to learning, we need to consider the pedagogical frame-work in terms of teacher–pupil interaction, curriculum, classroom physical environment, classroom discussions within which ICT is used. A fundamental question is not whether but how ICT should be used to support teacher–pupil and pupil–pupil interactions and contribute to inclusive learning. As an early year practitioner, you need to think about the function of ICT in the whole school and your classroom, and ensure that ICT fits with current curricular structures and the school's technical infrastructure. In a study by Ertmer and her colleagues three levels of computer use were identified, with ICT being

1   a supplement to the curriculum (e.g. using ICT for entertainment purposes mainly);
2   a reinforcement or enrichment of the current curriculum (e.g. using ICT to teach phonics as a part of a reading programme for pupils with dyslexia or to enrich/ extend the curriculum for gifted pupils); and
3   a facilitator of the curriculum (e.g. supporting young children with emerging literacy skills) (1999).

## ICT and early years practitioners: barriers and facilitators

It is important to note that what makes technology work is the human factor, with regard to whether users perceive ICT to be facilitative, relevant and capable of being implemented in a socially and educationally constructive way. Effective use of ICT is linked to the practitioners' beliefs and attitudes regarding its usefulness, their confidence in using it and the availability of good technical support. If you, as a practitioner, are an ICT novice, you would need to prepare yourself to learn through trial and error, be willing to admit that you lack technical knowledge and, most importantly, be flexible to change the way you teach to make a more widespread use of ICT.

Current ICT developments are likely to have a positive effect on staff training and development. This is particularly important in the face of growing concerns that early years practitioners are offered limited training and support to develop professionally. Over the years, there have been a number of governmental initiatives that encourage the use of ICT as a training, learning and inclusion tool to facilitate professional development and support pupils' learning. The British Educational and Communication Technology Agency (Becta) was formed in 1998 with the aim to support teachers who teach SEN pupils by accessing information and networking with other colleagues. Becta has put a number of systems in place, such as mailing lists and an electronic discussion forum for teachers, and has also developed databases to enable teachers who teach pupils with SEN to find information about teaching strategies and access resources and materials. The New Opportunities Fund has also provided training, information and resources to increase teachers' confidence to teach pupils with SEN (Stevens, 2004). Finally, the Teacher Training Agency has developed a CD-ROM to help teachers assess SEN pupils' needs and requirements for accessing the curriculum in the mainstream.

Jones conducted a survey for and on behalf of Becta to identify the obstacles that teachers typically encounter in using ICT (Becta, 2004). The results revealed, consistently with previous studies (e.g. Snoeyink and Ertmer, 2001), the existence of 'external and internal barriers' that prevent teachers from making full use of ICT in their classrooms (2004: 2). External barriers refer to those that result from poor organisational structures and leadership within an organisation or institution. Specifically, limited resources and lack of time and technical support are the most commonly stated external factors that impede an effective ICT use in an organisation (Becta, 2004).

Internal barriers refer to the individual users' characteristics such as age, willingness to undertake risks, motivation, perception of the benefits using ICT, resistance to change teaching styles and the overall attitudes towards technology (Becta, 2004). A key finding in Becta study is the link between ICT use and individual teachers' level of confidence. Specifically, teachers who have limited confidence in using computers in their work will try to avoid them altogether (Dawes, 2000; Russell and Bradley, 1997). Limited ICT use was also explained by the degree of ICT access that teachers have (Guha, 2000), access to technical support available (Cuban, 1999) and the amount and quality of training offered (Lee, 1997).

The literature organises classroom strategies to support teachers and other practitioners to use ICT into two main areas, namely school-based and externally supported strategies (Scrimshaw, 2004). It is important to acknowledge that many factors are likely to affect the use of ICT that should be explored at an individual and an organisational level.

### Individual level

The findings from a survey by Scrimshaw identified certain factors that enable staff to use ICT. These include

- access to own personal laptop and software
- availability of high quality resources
- high level of technical support
- access to an interactive whiteboard and
- availability of good quality training (2004: 12).

Specifically, teachers stated that having a personal laptop with appropriate software programmes is enabling, in that they are not constrained to prepare their teaching in the classroom or at school. It also helps them to organise diverse functions, such as lesson planning, keeping organisational lists of assignments and accessing pupils' records. To feel confident in using ICT, teachers require good ICT training to increase their technical knowledge and alleviate potential technophobias. They also need on-site technical support that is readily available whenever something goes wrong in the middle of a lesson or during consultation meetings with parents.

### Organisational level

Educational reforms rely on innovative practice and leadership to enable teachers and other classroom staff to engage and implement technological innovations. Scrimshaw (2004) conducted a thorough review of the ways in which schools use ICT in classrooms. He identified three elements of planning, at an organisational level, that are likely to enable educators to implement and manage change with regard to ICT use. These are a vision statement reflecting schools' philosophy and ethos; a needs assessment to evaluate existing resources and infrastructure to inform decision-making; and a school development plan with clear goals and objectives. These findings suggest that a whole-school approach should be taken when decisions about access to ICT are made, ensuring that teachers and other staff have the opportunity to express their views and contribute to the development of ICT plans.

Furthermore, Scrimshaw (2004) stressed the importance of schools drawing on outside support to improve their use of ICT. This can be achieved by working closely with the local community and agencies to offer reliable technical and social network support in schools. Nursery managers, in particular, are likely to welcome further links with the community in that early years education is influenced by the children's family and the surrounding community. External support should also be provided to early years staff in the form of locally based training opportunities geared towards continu- ous professional development, and through participation in national ICT initiatives and training schemes.

## ICT enabling early years staff

Electronic networks and discussion internet groups, such as the Foundation Stage Forum, are great resources for early years practitioners to keep up to date with ICT developments, obtain information about good practice, access resources, engage in discussions with peers and boost their confidence to use ICT. The Foundation Stage Forum in particular is an excellent community resource for those involved in early years education in that it creates an online community where nursery staff and reception teachers interact with each other and other child practitioners to offer and seek advice and share resources and examples of good practice.

There is a growing consensus that ICT has tremendous potential for enabling early years practitioners in particular to provide good quality of education and care for all children including those with SEN and, most importantly, strengthening home–school communica- tion and parental involvement. Specifically, ICT can enable educators to deliver the curric- ulum in a consistent manner across classroom settings, help parents access information readily and encourage inter-professional collaboration by providing mutual support to try new schemes and make the necessary changes in their teaching approaches.

With regard to home–school partnerships, as I discuss in the next chapter, close links between early years practitioners and families are crucial for effective early years educa- tion with ICT making an important contribution to strengthening home–school partner- ships. ICT can be used in a number of ways to facilitate good working relationships between schools and parents. Specifically, parents may obtain information about their children by accessing school records from home, keep an open communication channel with teachers via the use of email and access/share learning resources to meet their chil- dren's learning needs. All these functions are feasible given that, over the last years, there has been an enormous increase in home-ownership of computers.

Availability of home computers also encourages children to have an early start in using computers and extends their familiarisation with ICT beyond the school day. In this context, ICT use has a positive effect on young children's readiness to embrace technology and use it constructively. There is evidence of pupil motivation and engage- ment in ICT-based tasks, particularly when such work is undertaken at home without the constraints of time and the classroom environment. Young children can use ICT to continue their work at home without interruption.

## Classroom-based ICT strategies: enabling pupils with dyslexia

In this section, several recommendations are discussed with regard to classroom ICT use to support learning in young children with dyslexia. The focus of the ICT-based methods presented here is on phonological skills development, word-level work (spelling, word recognition, handwriting) and sentence/text level work (writing, reading comprehension) consistent with the NLS framework (see Chapter 5 for a discussion of

NLS). The computer-based programmes discussed in this section are chosen because they make appropriate demands on young children with dyslexia, and can be used in the context of teacher–pupil interactions. A teacher-aided use of ICT, especially when tasks or games are introduced, enables pupils to use it as a learning tool. Also, the presence of teachers or learning support assistants is needed to provide feedback; for example, during phonic work, teachers need to facilitate children's oral responses to the screen prompts to ensure that they make correct letter–sound correspondences.

Up until fairly recently, the use of ICT had focused on children with physical disabilities and communication difficulties. It is only in the last years that ICT has spread among children with other SEN, including dyslexia. For young children with dyslexia who are likely to experience difficulties with reading, phonological skills, spelling and writing, including handwriting, the use of ICT is likely to alleviate the impact of these difficulties on learning. ICT allows children to work at their own pace, without worrying about poor handwriting, messy presentation and mistakes in sounding out/deciphering new words. Also, using ICT to develop basic literacy and numeracy skills in young children can be motivating in terms of boosting their self-esteem and encouraging them to become independent learners. Game-based programmes on screen stimulate young children in ways that print does not, offering them opportunities for consolidating their learning through repetition and trial and error.

The literature on ICT use during teaching and learning focuses almost exclusively on primary and secondary education. ICT use in early years settings is at its initial stages of development, partly because young children at nursery and reception are less likely to use ICT as a tool for accessing information from the internet to support their academic work. Rather, they tend to use computers for fun activities and, possibly, for practising and consolidating emergent literacy skills.

Early exposure to ICT enables children to become independent learners capable of accessing information to facilitate their learning. However, it is important to note that ICT use should be mediated by social interactions where children have the opportunity to discuss computer-based tasks, engage in critical thinking and construct knowledge that is mediated by social experiences. There is an ongoing criticism with regard to the pedagogies that underlie the use of ICT, especially for young children. Children who use technology in a way that is not mediated and enriched by human experience through teacher–pupil interactions and peer collaborative learning activities are likely to become passive recipients/consumers of information with limited capacity for critical analysis and thinking. For ICT use to extend learning beyond traditional boundaries, its pedagogical context should be one that encourages independent thinking, autonomous learning, self-direction and self-monitoring, ability to engage in problem solving and co-operative learning.

Young children with dyslexia are likely to benefit from ICT use in that it

- enables them to take control of their own learning, encouraging a degree of independence
- increases the time spent for hands-on activities
- raises self-esteem and self-confidence
- encourages them to actively search for answers to questions posed
- maximises incidental learning
- makes them gain practical experience with regard to planning and monitoring their work
- removes obstacles related to dyslexia, such as poor handwriting and slow writing pace
- allows them to practice and over-learn basic skills such as phonics and

• supports the use of language and communication skills by encouraging children to talk about computer-based tasks, explaining what they do to other pupils and engaging in discussions with teachers.

There are numerous computer software programmes designed to support pupils with dyslexia with regard to phonological development, spelling, writing, reading and handwriting through multi-sensory teaching that combines computer games with learning to read and spell. These games use sound, graphic and text to teach word recognition and spelling. There are also software programmes designed to support handwriting in terms of teaching the correct siting position, paper position and pen holding. Handwriting computer programmes include alphabet cards in an electronic format that can be viewed and printed to help young pupils improve the style, legibility and fluency of their handwriting.

### Phonology computer programmes

As I discussed in previous chapters, phonological development is crucial for deciphering and recognising words, reading and writing. Computer-based programmes designed to raise phonological awareness rely primarily on building the sounds of the English language. They start from developing a basic understanding of consonant-vowel-consonant (c-v-c) sequences, to functional phonological skills (blending sounds, diagraphs) to, ultimately, independent decoding of multi-syllable words. The majority of phonological programmes combine independent work with the computer in the context of receiving guidance from reception teachers or learning support assistants to ensure that the links between sounds and letters are formed correctly.

Effective phonic programmes are those that do not encourage rote memorisation of words, by emphasising phonic rules from which pupils are able to generalise and transfer phonological knowledge across literacy tasks, e.g. reading, spelling and writing. These programmes are designed to teach syllable segmention and blending where pupils look at the word and can hear it spoken simultenously. They can be used in the context of whole-classroom or dyadic teacher–pupil interactions, encouraging both collaborative and independent learning. Children find computer-based phonic exercises more preferable than paper ones in that they allow for different colours or fonts to be used as a visual aid to discriminate various parts of a word, e.g. root words or word endings.

The *InSound* is a Key Stage 1 phonics programme used at a whole-class level, designed to benefit all children, particularly those with dyslexia. It is suitable for children in Reception or Year 1, as well as for older pupils who need to practice phonics in terms of relating sounds to letters and vice versa. This computer-aided programme contains fifteen units of work that can be spread over three terms, within the context of the NLS. In a similar fashion, *Making Sense with Letters* helps with phonics and word building by using graphics and sound. It supports children finding the initial phoneme (the smallest unit of sound), fill in the missing letter in the middle of words (medial phoneme) and unscramble the letters that comprise words.

These phonic programmes are designed to support reading, spelling and writing through the development of phonological skills, including sound segmentation and blending, rhyming, awareness of the position of letters and the corresponding phonemes in a word (initial or medial). They also support the development of letter knowledge in the alphabet, spelling rules and patterns, and making connections between reading and writing. The presence of teachers or learning support assistants is essential to make these programmes work effectively, especially with phonic work, where children's responses need to be checked and reinforced by the teachers to ensure that the links they make between letters and sounds are correct.

### Working memory computer programmes

There are computer-based programmes that include exercises to improve children's short-term memory and the capacity to transfer information to long-term memory and retrieve it when needed. Some memory programmes use a sequence of pictures of animals, food, transport and other items that children are asked to memorise. The pictures are presented visually and auditorially to improve visual and auditory sequential memory.

There is a CD-ROM developed by the BBC in conjunction with leading European experts in the field of dyslexia called *The Mystery of the Lost Letters* (www.tosuccess. org.uk) for pupils aged seven to thirteen and their tutors and parents. This can also be used as a diagnostic tool to provide information about how individual pupils learn and their profile of strengths and weaknesses, offering advice on how to cope with weaknesses.

### Language computer programmes

Young children with dyslexia who present language difficulties can benefit from software programmes that support the development of receptive and expressive language. The following is a list of Windows software programmes designed to support language.

*On the Farm* – This is designed for early years pupils to develop language skills, perceptual/sequential skills and literacy skills (word building). All the activities are accessible with a mouse, touch monitor, keyboard or switches. Children can work as a group to

- build up a farm scene, by selecting one picture at a time
- change the position of pictures/objects
- see and/or hear the word that accompanies objects in a scene and
- label a scene by using the words given.

This programme mainly helps children develop the concept of foreground and background and the vocabulary that goes with it (e.g. behind, front), as well as knowledge about the semantic (meaning) and the pragmatic aspects of language by learning vocabulary words and placing them into the social context they are used (i.e. farm scene). Pupils are able to actively construct different scenes and create different stories to share with the group, maximising the creative use of language.

*Picture Sentence Key* – This is designed to enable children with expressive language difficulties develop basic phrases by teaching the concept of 'who is doing what'. Children with expressive language difficulties find grouping words together to express meaning challenging. This programme supports the development of grammar and syntax when putting words together, in that there is a 'who' list which contains the pictures of five people, a 'doing' list which contains six verbs and a 'what' list which contains nineteen items. Children can use these lists in any combination and explore the different ways words are placed in a sentence to make meaning.

*Switchit! Opposites* – This Windows software stimulates the development of both the receptive and expressive language skills by teaching children the concept of opposites, such as big/little, up/down, in/out, open/closed and hot/cold. Both text and speech are used to help children link print with spoken language.

*Foundation Counting Songs* – It introduces young children to popular counting songs (e.g. Five Green Bottles, Ten Little Ducks, Ten Currant Buns in a Bakers Shop) with animation and music. This can be used in a group or an individual basis and is designed to support the language used in maths.

*Spider in the Kitchen* – This software is designed to support the development of spatial language, positional words in particular, by teaching children to match objects to suitable locations. Positional words such as behind, above, below, beside, in or on are practised by using familiar objects and locations.

### Writing/handwriting computer programmes

*Writing with Symbols* – This Windows 95 programme was designed to support children with writing difficulties by pairing visual aids (e.g. pictures) with words. Children as young as four can write by selecting words, pictures or any combination of the two. There is a built-in speech facility to help children make links between the words they see and the sounds that comprise them. This programme teaches writing in a multi-sensory manner by utilising different modalities, e.g. visual, auditory, when presenting words.

*I can Write* – This programme provides the structure that young children with writing difficulties need to put words together into paper. It allows them to write about any topic they like by clicking the images and responding to questions. At a more advanced level, they may use themed text prompts and word banks and build their own story.

Computer-aided handwriting can be particulalry facilitative in that touch screens help pupils to 'follow' the letter shape, directionality and joining strokes. Also, as Cooke (2002) points out, using keyboards is a kineasthetic experience in itself that reinforces the learning of spelling patterns through motor memory. In terms of self-esteem, children with poor handwriting are likey to feel 'not as good as their peers'. Thus, the use of computers, which allow them to work at their own pace and produce good quality outputs, is likely to increase their motivation.

### Reading and spelling computer programmes

*My World* (Reading and Recording) is a series of programmes to support the development of early literacy skills. They are designed for early years teachers and learning support assistants to provide structured reading activities. They can be used to support children with diverse needs, and are operated at word, sentence and text level. Children with dyslexia who are likely to present difficulties at the word, sentence or text level when encountering literacy tasks can benefit from this programme. With *My World*, Children practice spelling, word or letter matching, cloze activities (i.e. leaving sentences incomplete, inviting children to choose the right word to complete them), writing from memory and phonics. These programmes include:

*My World* (Three-Letter Words) helps children develop matching and reading skills of three-letter words. Also, *My World* story book is a good starting point for children to make their own story book by using images and words appropriate to Goldilocks, Three Pigs and Red Riding Hood. This is a fun way of developing storytelling skills, which can be daunting for many young children in that they require an advanced use of language.

At the word level, *Making Sense with Words* allows children to complete sentences by responding to coloured images with speech support. It provides a wide range of sentences to be formed by using verbs, nouns, prepositions, articles, colours and spelling in imaginative ways.

At the sentence level, 'talking books' on a computer are very good for enhancing listening and reading comprehension skills, especially for young children with dyslexia who experience difficulties sounding out and recognising words, resulting in restricted reading. Children should be aided to listen to the whole story guided by the cursor to make links between sounds and words. Cooke (2002) suggests a number of computer-based reading books including the *Oxford Reading Tree*, *Fuzz Buzz* and *Cambridge Reading* to enhance children's ability to extract meaning from text.

### Communication and information

*Internet and the Web* – Although this multimedia function is suitable for older children, pupils in Y1 and Y2 may benefit from starting developing ways of searching the internet and sending emails to friends and family members. Many households have access to computers nowadays and, thus, some children may have already been exposed to and practised these functions. Locating information in the internet is likely to facilitate reading, whereas sending emails to friends can motivate a dyslexic child to write. Also, there is a degree of tolerance built in these systems in that the main purpose of sending an email is to communicate with another person, thus, spelling and grammatical errors as well as lack of conventions of writing are tolerated, alleviating some of the pressure that literacy difficulties pose on children with dyslexia.

## Summary

Information Communication Technology holds immense potential for supporting teaching and learning in young children. ICT is increasingly seen as a tool for inclusion in terms of supporting children with SEN to learn in the mainstream, and for professional development by introducing early years practitioners to good practice, and assisting them in accessing resources and expertise with regard to early years education through the internet and discussion fora. We know that what makes technology work is the human factor; thus, early years practitioners should be supported to develop the confidence required to use ICT effectively. The developmental appropriateness of ICT use and its pedagogic framework have been extensively critiqued, stressing the need for mediating children's ICT use through social interactions with teachers, parents and peers. The use of ICT is expanding from children with physical disabilities and communication problems to those with dyslexia and other learning difficulties. There have been numerous computer-based programmes designed to support children with dyslexia to acquire literacy skills at the word, sentence and text level, enhance their motivation and stimulate them in ways that print does not. A fundamental issue, however, that early years practitioners should raise is whether children with dyslexia are able to transfer the knowledge and skills acquired through ICT into the non-virtual world of the classroom.

# Chapter 7

# Working with parents and other professionals

## Introduction

During the 1970s and 1980s, educational researchers and practitioners used to describe teaching as the 'lonely profession' in that, up until then, the understanding was that teachers have the sole responsibility for catering for pupils' learning and pastoral development. The 1990s brought with them notions of teamwork, inter-professional collaboration, parental involvement and rights, professional standards and account-ability, all placing different demands on teachers and other educational practitioners. The increasing professionalisation of teachers has shifted their identities, roles and responsibilities to become more responsive to client needs and demands by developing working relationships with both the providers and the receivers of educational services (Menter *et al.*, 1997).

This chapter is organised in two sections. The first section focuses on early years practitioners' contact with parents of young children with SEN, including dyslexia, in terms of formal consultation meetings, collaborative workings as well as informal interactions. A number of legislative frameworks (e.g. SEN Code of Practice, home–school partnerships) have reinforced the importance of parents' rights and parental involvement in their children's education, stimulating further interactions between parents and practitioners. The second section looks at early years teachers/staff working with learning support assistants, SENCOS and other adults in the classroom, as well as outside professionals and agencies. There has been a lot written about deploying additional adult support in the classroom to alleviate some of the pressure teachers experience and encourage inclusive practices. There is, however, an ongoing debate about the role of the learning support assistants and other adults in the classroom and the quality of their interactions with teachers, as well as issues regarding training and inter-professional collaboration.

## Home–school partnerships

Early years staff are increasingly expected to form close links with parents and encourage them to become actively involved in their children's education. Since 1999, setting up home–school partnerships and agreements has become obligatory by law. These agreements are placed in the context of the school ethos, reach-out policies with the surrounding community, pupil attendance and parental participation, especially for minority ethnic parents and extended family members through liaison officers and translators.

The revised SEN Code of Practice (DfES, 2001) also stresses the importance of parental participation in the decision-making for children's education. Parents are increasingly seen as capable of fulfilling multiple roles in terms of

- providing first-hand information regarding their children's learning and development;
- expressing their own wishes and convictions regarding their children's education;
- engaging in decision-making regarding the provision of SEN services; and
- ensuring consistency with regard to the implementation of intervention strategies by adopting them at home and providing feedback about their effectiveness for follow-up considerations.

A large number of research studies indicate that parental support of children's reading in particular is critical during their early education years (e.g. Anderson, 1992; Singh *et al.*, 1992). Parents, regardless of their reading skills, are effective in helping their children read as long as they are responsive and 'dialogic' with their children during shared reading, by talking about text and drawing links between ideas and children's experiences (Henderson and Berla, 1994).

Understanding the nature of practitioner–parent relationships has important implications for young children's education and care. Cunningham and Davis (1985) offered different views to explain the interaction between educational practitioners and parents and the roles they assume. Specifically, some parents see themselves as being the passive recipients of educational services and the practitioners as the main source of knowledge and expertise. Others may view this relationship as being interactive with both parents and professionals working together to provide expertise and resources to support children's learning and ensure continuity of learning support at home.

## Working with parents: diverse perspectives and views

Awareness among early years practitioners about various family practices, values and functions and the ways they are influenced by ethnic, social and economic factors are important for building successful home–school partnerships. It is a balancing act for every educator to consider the views of parents and other professionals, and those of the children themselves, and ensure that the children's best interests are safeguarded in a consistent and inclusive manner. Furthermore, it is crucial for early years practitioners to find effective ways to exchange information about children's educational needs and progress, encourage parental involvement and establish a mutually respectful and supportive relationship with parents (McBride *et al.*, 2001).

There are many aspects of diversity with regard to parents' social, cultural and ethnic backgrounds, influencing the ways they interact with professionals. We think about diversity mainly when we encounter parents from different ethnic and religious back-grounds, in that ethnicity and religion constitute visible markers of difference. It is possible, however, to underestimate diversity in parents whom we perceive to be part of the mainstream society. The following case studies illustrate different types of parental involvement (or lack of it) and parent–practitioner relationships with parents from diverse social-cultural and ethnic backgrounds. Some of the examples presented here are based on Riddell, Wilson, Adler and Mordaunt's descriptive framework of parent–educator collaborative workings (2002).

---

### Case study 1

Disengaged parent, marginalised due to a deeply rooted social exclusion and suspicion towards the educational system and its agents.

Lucy is four years old and lives with her parents in a council house in a socially and economically deprived area. Lucy was born prematurely, and from early on, her mother realised that there is something 'wrong with her'. By the time she joined the nursery she had serious language difficulties with her speech being intelligible, co-ordination difficulties in terms of gross motor skills (i.e. unco-ordinated running) and fine motor skills (i.e. difficulties tying up her shoe laces, using knife and fork properly and holding the pencil correctly). Also, socially, she appeared to be immature and easily excitable, preferring the company of younger children. Academically, she presents difficulties learning the alphabet, drawing, forming letters and using language during classroom discussions. She also experiences serious difficulties with maths in terms of understanding simple mathematical concepts and counting, getting confused when counting with her fingers. Overall, her academic performance and social development are far behind compared to that of her peers.

---

Assume that this pupil joins your reception class without any formal assessment to delineate her learning profile and needs. Her parents have been contacted for a meeting and, when they are asked about their daughter's developmental and school history, they state that Lucy has always been a 'bit behind' without providing a detailed developmental history to help you piece together this child's strengths and weaknesses. The school carries out an assessment and concerns about dyspraxia are raised with the recommendation of involving an occupational therapist and a speech and language therapist to alleviate Lucy's difficulties with motor co-ordination and language development.

At the end of your first meeting with Lucy's parents, you ask them to come back after the assessment to discuss the results and the recommendations regarding SEN provision. You find that communicating with them is not easy, and feel that the trust in the parent–professional relationship is missing, possibly because Lucy's parents had had negative previous experiences dealing with schools and other public institutions/ organisations in the past, resulting in feelings of alienation and mistrust. It is also possible that Lucy's parents have experienced learning difficulties themselves and had reduced educational opportunities, all contributing to being passive consumers of educational services. Regardless of the reasons for the apparent mistrust, it will take time and a lot of effort on your part to build trust and encourage them to become involved actively in their child's education.

**Case study 2**

Parents as active consumers of services in a market-driven education

Julia is a six-year-old daughter of professional parents with high educational aspirations. She appears articulate and mature for her age. Verbally, she is a confident speaker who always participates in classroom discussions and interacts with her peers properly. She enjoys being read to and has a good comprehension of text. She likes re-telling stories by engaging in detailed accounts. However, she finds it very difficult to understand and make links between sounds and letters and sound out simple words. When she attempts to sound out unknown words, she either pronounces the wrong letters altogether or substitutes them with another word that starts with the same letter. Spelling is equally poor with a number of letter reversals being noted. Handwriting also presents serious difficulties in terms of poor letter size and directionality and slow pace.

Julia's parents are aware of the literacy difficulties their daughter has been experiencing since reception, and have been pro-active in terms of requesting for an assessment to ensure that the necessary educational provision is in place. They have also had a private assessment, corroborating the diagnosis of dyslexia, and have accessed private tutoring to supplement the learning support provided at school. Julia's parents are keen on visiting the school and meeting with you and the SENCO. They feel that they exercise their right for choice in terms of choosing the services they deem appropriate for Julia. Choice has become a contentious term in that, for parents and families who are marginalised, choice is more likely to be forced upon them rather than exercised. On the other hand, for parents, like Julia's, who have the market power and are able to locate and access the services they want, choice is exercised fully.

**Case study 3**

Parents as activists and advocates of their children's rights

John was three and a half when he was diagnosed with Asperger's syndrome (autistic spectrum disorder). When he started reception his speech was limited and also displayed some behavioural difficulties. His parents were adamant that he attended the village school (mainstream). At reception, the teacher described him as 'non-verbal' in that he could not engage in question-and-answer interactions. Consequently, when his teacher asked him 'What is your name?' or 'Would you like to play with a ball?' he did not know how to answer. The parents felt that the information obtained by the teacher during her interactions with John is not adequate and perhaps somewhat misleading. In an attempt to provide more information about John's language use, the parents tape-recorded him talking while watching his parents drawing a picture, saying 'Mommy and Daddy can make the puppy be eating a dog biscuit!'

John's parents felt that the teacher's description of their son as being 'non-verbal' was not accurate and, thus, they provided the teacher with evidence regarding his use of language during family interactions. They also raised awareness about the implications of misunderstanding their son's social and linguistic functioning, and in collaboration with other professionals, they requested that an educational psychologist assesses their child's communicative skills at their home. The educational psychologist was willing to assess John at home, and also interviewed neighbours who had interacted with John to cross-examine information about his linguistic and social behaviour.

There was a great deal of stress placed upon John's parents to apply behaviour modification strategies to make John participate in tasks in classroom. The parents felt that behaviour modification was not 'right for their son' in that they could see how distressing it was to ask him to change his plans without understanding the underlying reasons for doing so. The parents visited him at school (reception class) and observed him in classroom 'calmly playing with tape recorders, making pictures, looking at books, though not at the same time as the other children', and 'felt that his behaviour in school was fine'. However, the teacher told parents that they 'should make him do more things'. John's parents accounts of the role of the learning support teacher has as follows:

> Our son was given a full-time support teacher who dragged him from one activity to the next. Not understanding the reasons, he would struggle against her and laugh. There were frequent meetings with a psychiatrist from the council, who did understand a lot, but who could do little more in a few hours than give advice about specific problems as they may arise. There was no way for us, as parents, to challenge the whole model of what education should mean to a child.

John's parents approached the teacher and explained what it means to ask an autistic-spectrum child to do something without having any understanding as to why he is asked. Through an open dialogue with the teacher, John's parents were able to express their worries and needs. However, they felt that ascertaining their child's rights within what they perceived to be an 'inflexible education system' was a perpetual struggle.

The last case study illustrates a number of issues that are likely to arise during parent–teacher interactions, including teachers' limited evidence about children's linguistic and communicative functioning across a variety of contexts, difficulties in interpreting parents' anxieties and wishes and limited access to information held by other professionals. John's parents were involved in every step of the decision-making about their son's education. They were involved not as consumers of services but as advocates of their child's rights, willing to collaborate with the professionals and facilitate their work. They had the knowledge and the insight of their son's functioning, and were able to communicate their intimate understanding effectively.

The main difference between the last two cases of parental involvement, i.e. parents as active consumers of services and parents as activists and advocates, is that the latter type of parents do not perceive education as a set of services that are delivered to their children passively. Rather, they see themselves as co-constructing educational experiences and provision that is right for their child in the context of a dynamic and equal collaboration with the professionals. John's parents did not exercise choice in ways that parents as service consumers do; instead, they negotiated access to provision and were willing to put the time and the effort necessary to ensure the implementation of proper educational provision. They also have the social and cultural capital and the insight to be advocates for their children's rights without restricting their role to that of being a passive consumer of educational services.

The three case studies presented here encapsulate the experiences of parents of children with SEN in their interactions with teachers and other professionals. They do not necessarily constitute mutually exclusive categories, although parents who experience social exclusion and marginalisation are less likely to form collaborative links with teachers and other professionals and become actively involved in their children's education and advocates of their children's rights. Also, rapid changes in today's family structure and value systems continue to shape home–school partnerships and parent–professional collaborative workings in ways that are not always easily understood. In this changing climate, early years practitioners need to re-think about parental involvement, family structures and parents' roles and responsibilities.

## The new face of families

The changing face of families and, most importantly, the changing nature of parent–child relationships is likely to affect the ways in which early years staff relate to and work with parents. In a market-driven society, the provision of care and education is judged by the criteria of a consumer society, namely choice, variety, disposability and competitiveness. The emphasis on choice has changed parents' views of their involvement in their children's education, as well as their expectations about teachers' and school staff's standards of work and accountability. Parents increasingly feel that they are in a position to choose the best care and education for their children, a good value for their money in a competitive market where schools and teachers are perceived as being 'service providers'. In this context, some parents see themselves as the main decision makers in terms of selecting the educational services they deem appropriate for their children.

Changes in today's families and parental roles and responsibilities have all contributed to re-defining parent–professional partnerships. Families gradually become smaller and smaller, with a growing trend for extended families to become marginalised and nuclear families to become isolated. The number of one-parent families increases. Pre-school children spend less and less time with their parents, and the provision of care is increasingly seen as another type of 'service' for which parents need to 'sub-contract' others to provide it. For many parents, spending time with their children has become a 'bonus', instead of something they naturally do, impacting on the quality of parent–child relationships. As Martin Jacques (2004) comments in an article published in *The Guardian* newspaper, the deterioration in parent–child relationship 'should alarm us the most'. For more than a century, theorists in the field of psychology and education have stressed the importance of the emotional bonds between parents and children as the basis for our emotional and linguistic development, socialisation and learning, as well as our very sense of 'being human' (28).

The lack of time and opportunity to interact with young children has affected the very fabric of intimacy between parents and children. Jacques argues that children grow up with their experiences being 'mediated through the media' and not through personal contact with their families and communities, resulting in limited real-life experiences (2004: 28). The consequences of the decline in parent–child interactions have become increasingly apparent as the results from a survey by the Basic Skills Agency (2003) revealed that a large number of reception children display poor language and communication skills, having a knock-on effect on their emotional maturity, social skills and learning. With such a start in life, it is likely that some children will experience a range of behavioural and emotional difficulties and, probably, a reduced capacity for learning.

Despite the decline in parent–children interactions, the most important social-emotional and communicative experiences for the majority of children still occur within their family. Snow *et al.* (1998) stressed the need for parents, caregivers and early years professionals to interact with children in terms of having conversations with them, reading books, providing writing materials and introducing dramatic play and literacy activities in a playful manner. It is widely accepted that successful intervention strategies regarding children's learning and development are achieved through caregiver–professional partnerships. Specifically, the implementation of family-based 'primary prevention' schemes is becoming increasingly prominent. However, it is important to note that when designing early years interventions to be carried out in a family context or by family members, the beliefs and values of the family, as well as the stress and challenges they face should be considered.

## Meeting with parents: consultation events

Consultation meetings can take many forms. They may be teacher- or parent-initiated, can take place anytime during the school day or in the evening, and may or may not involve the pupils. A successful consultation meeting requires preparation on your part by accumulating the necessary background information, and an insight into what parents might want to achieve from it by taking their perspectives and wishes into account. The parents may need information and advice about specific aspects of their children's learning and social development, or raise issues they feel should be addressed at school, or simply, they may need to be re-assured. Awareness of the factors that are likely to shape parent–teacher interactions, such as diversity in perspectives and approaches and family values and beliefs, is crucial to make consultation meetings a worthwhile experience for all involved.

For a consultation meeting, you need to prepare in terms of

- collecting all the necessary materials (Individualised Education Plans for SEN pupils, assessment reports, SENCO's statements) that are relevant to the case;
- gathering and organising information obtained from existing school documents and/or other professionals involved;
- having information cross-examined before presenting it to the parents; for example, you may need to talk with the learning support assistant and/or SENCO before the meeting to ensure that the information you have is accurate and consistent with existing records;
- providing parents with ways of helping their children at home by making suggestions about helping children with homework, e.g. strategies to teach times tables, phonics;
- devising a tentative framework for action that is flexible and capable of incorporating the conclusions drawn during the meeting; and
- setting up follow-up meetings and procedures to ensure that action is taken and evaluate its outcomes.

You may also encourage parents to prepare for the meeting by asking them to

- write down specific questions they may have about their children with regard to class behaviour, concentration, homework, particular strengths or peer interactions;
- provide them with all the information they need during the meeting in terms of delineating the areas of difficulties, e.g. Which times table is the pupil having trouble with? Is there a certain time of day when a child acts out? and
- discuss their overall concerns with regard to their children's learning and social-emotional development.

Throughout the meeting, ensure that parents have opportunities to talk without being interrupted. Their input is crucial in that they have an intimate knowledge and a good understanding about their children's developmental and learning needs. Regardless of whether or not children are present during the meeting, it is important to have a discussion with them in simple terms, about the issues raised during the meeting and the proposed plan for action, although with very young children this may not always be possible.

During consultation meetings, parents are likely to experience a wide range of emotions, including nervousness, anxiety, feelings of guilt, alienation and unhappiness. It is important to defuse negative emotions from the start by being positive about their children, pointing out areas of strength, making helpful suggestions, stating facts accurately and being aware of your own assumptions and biases. Expect to see diversity in parents' perspectives with regard to how they view their role in their children's education, especially with parents from minority ethnic backgrounds. As I already mentioned, parents from certain cultures and social backgrounds may perceive teaching as the sole responsibility of the teacher with them having a minimum input, if any at all. Understanding diversity is crucial to enable you dispel myths and assumptions that are likely to underlie your interaction with parents and communicate with them clearly.

After the meeting, it is a good practice to provide parents with a written report. It is crucial that the information included is accurate and cross-examined with other pieces of evidence. The report should also be balanced in terms of stating strengths and weaknesses, and inclusive with regard to taking into consideration pupils' learning, language and social and emotional development. The law requires that schools provide written reports on pupils' progress at least once each academic year. At the foundation stage, the written report should include:

- a delineation of the pupils' strengths and areas of development needs;
- general views on their progress; and
- information on attendance (authorised and unauthorised).

It is also important to set the stage for ongoing communication with parents and plan future meetings. Ongoing communication can be achieved by encouraging parents to

- implement classroom strategies at home
- check their child's homework routinely
- identify areas of improvement and point out areas of weakness
- suggest ways to work with you in the future on a regular basis. For example, you could write each other notes or talk on the phone and
- involve their children by letting them know about the discussions they had with you.

The key to successful home-school partnerships is to provide parents with the information, guidance, consistent feedback and encouragement to enable them to provide at home what their children need to succeed in school. Children's school achievement can significantly improve when parents, regardless of their socio-economic position, encourage pre-literacy and literacy activities (e.g. storytelling, reading) at home, and are aware of the school-related learning activities (Wang *et al.*, 1993a).

A number of studies by Wang, Walberg and their colleagues in the USA suggest that the family environment is particularly powerful in influencing children's academic achievement. Walberg coined the phrase 'curriculum of the home' to refer to family behaviours, lifestyles, values and expectations that are more predictive of children's school success than socio-economic status (1984). According to Walberg and his colleagues, the curriculum of the home involves homework, family reading sessions, parents' communication patterns with teachers, the routine of family life, monitoring of TV watching and, most importantly, parental aspirations/expectations for children's academic achievement. These findings challenge prevalent notions that children's social-cultural capital and academic achievement are intrinsically linked to their family's financial standing (see Introduction for a detailed discussion on social-cultural capital and its links with academic achievement).

## Working with other professionals: a diverse workforce

Child development is multi-faceted and thus mono-disciplinary perspectives are not sufficient to address the complex nature of teaching and learning. As an educator, you are bound to work within an increasingly diverse workforce, alongside with a wide range of other professionals. To support children's learning in an effective and accountable manner, it is crucial to understand other professionals' roles, feel confident to take part in consultation sessions or informal interactions with them and develop good communication and negotiation skills.

It has been long recognised that the demands on teachers' workload increase and, thus, new systems, e.g. classroom adults, have been introduced to support them. However, working with other adults in the classroom brings numerous challenges likely to overwhelm newly qualified teachers and early years staff. Forming collaborative workings with others requires you to re-examine your own values, beliefs, prejudices and assumptions, as well as work practices. This is likely to stimulate major shifts in the ways you teach which can be rather unsettling, causing uncertainty and anxiety. The use of teaching support staff to take on some of the teaching roles and responsibilities has been contentious, and a number of issues regarding training and efficient use of qualified teachers' time have been raised. On the positive side, working with colleagues may motivate you to open up to the scrutiny by your peers, and benefit from their constructive criticism. It may also stimulate you to become a life-long learner, above and beyond in-service training.

Undoubtedly, you and other educators will encounter various adults working in classrooms. These may be parent volunteers, experienced classroom or special needs assistants or qualified nursery nurses. Specialist Support Teachers normally provide support for children with SEN and for EAL children. Teaching assistants normally provide support to children who have fallen behind or those who are more able academically. Nursery assistants are often employed to provide support in Reception, particularly with children aged under five. Volunteer parents also provide invaluable support working with children on tasks set by the classroom teachers. Many classroom staff are experienced working with pupils, and can draw on their knowledge of the children and classroom activities. You as a teacher should remember, though, that however good your helpers are, it is your responsibility to direct and manage the learning process and the communication flow among classroom staff.

## Classroom staff: who are they?

In England and Wales, between 1997 and 2002 the number of teaching assistants or other support staff working in schools has doubled (Bills, 2004). The role of teaching and learning assistants has changed considerably over the last years. It started as a provision of practical support in the classroom, and has expanded to include responsibilities towards children's learning and development. These rapid changes have not always been followed by training and support, and although the National Primary Strategy (2003) addresses the training needs of classroom assistants, more needs to be done to support them perform their roles effectively. Training brings many challenges to learning assistants and also to you, as a reception/nursery staff, who works with them.

There are several terms used to describe adults working with teachers, causing confusion, potentially putting obstacles to inter-professional collaboration. Traditionally, the term 'paraprofessionals' has been used to describe non-qualified teachers or classroom assistants with no formal teaching qualifications. The term 'paraprofessionals' is contested, in that it differentiates some classroom staff from the 'professionals', without, however, delineating what their status is.

Bills (2004) provided a thorough description of some of the terms used to describe classroom staff by focusing on their roles and responsibilities. There are generic terms used, such as support staff, referring to those who are not qualified teachers (e.g. librarians, technicians, catering staff) and specific terms such as learning support assistants for those whose role is to support individual pupils or a group of pupils who display difficulties with learning. The term Teaching Assistant refers to those who directly support teachers in the classroom, whereas the term Classroom Assistant refers to adults who provide practical support in the classroom, e.g. passing books or other materials around, putting displays on the wall, tidying up after art.

Recently, there are two new roles added as a result of certain governmental initiatives. The first role is that of Learning Mentors derived from the governmental initiative 'Excellence in Cities', aiming at supporting pupils outside the school primarily, in terms of learning and social-emotional development. Also, the role of Ethnic Minority Achievement Grant Teacher and Assistant has been launched, employed to provide support to EAL pupils. Some of these professionals have expertise and knowledge in language development and are encouraged to work closely with families to maximise opportunities for language development.

## The role of Learning Support Assistants

Learning Support Assistants (LSA) is the most commonly used descriptions of adults working with teachers in classrooms. LSAs are now in almost all classrooms supporting children with SEN to learn in the mainstream. This is a general description of their role, with the specifics remaining as yet unclear, especially for early years education. There are several issues to be clarified, pertaining to the collaborative workings between nursery/reception teachers and LSAs, LSAs' training and professional development and the clarity of their roles and expectations. With regard to the last point, LSAs are seen as

- being attached to a particular child with SEN who receives learning support as a result of having a statement of SEN or being placed at the Early Years School Action or Early Years School Action Plus;
- overseeing a group of children working on a task set by the classroom teacher;
- withdrawing children to work on 1:1 or small groups to boost the development of specific skills, for example phonics in children with dyslexia.

Delineating LSAs' role is not straightforward in that it differs across classrooms and learning settings (e.g. early years, primary school). LSAs constitute a diverse workforce who are expected to support pupils' learning, pastoral development and behaviour, organise resources and materials and collaborate effectively with classroom teachers. More specifically, they are expecteed to facilitate learning by helping children before they engage in tasks set by the classroom teacher (preparation stage) and after they have completed a task by repeating newly acquired skills, such as the sounds of certain letters or the sequence of numbers (consolidation stage). Children with SEN often experience difficulties with their social and emotional development, as well as regulating their behaviour. For this group of children, LSAs' role also includes provision of pastoral support, e.g. boosting self-esteem and social skills, through modelling and coaching of pro-social behaviours.

The organisation of all these functions requires ongoing collaboration between LSAs and classroom teachers to ensure that appropriate discussions and negotiations take place. Developing successful collaborative workings between teachers and other adults in the classroom is not an easy undertaking. In the literature of inter-professional collaboration, limited communication and individual contribution, lack of organisational culture to support collaboration and lack of clarity in staff's roles and expectations have been found to pose obstacles towards inter-professional collaboration (Hartas, 2004).

## Working with outside agencies and professionals

Nursery and reception staff are expected to work with other professionals, such as Speech and Language Therapists, educational psychologists, and other specialists, through reciprocal consultation or direct instruction. Some classroom staff may lack the confidence and the training to support young children with SEN, e.g. dyslexia, in the mainstream. Their role and responsibilities have changed rapidly over the last years; often, they are required to deal with many new aspects of their job that lie outside their previous experience and training. In this context, they should be supported to meet their new job requirements through inter-professional collaboration, mentoring and consultation. Collaboration is a two-way street, with both teachers and other classroom staff undergoing significant personal and professional changes to work effectively with others. This is not an easy territory especially for classroom or learning assistants who may not be well equipped, in terms of training and professional development to undertake multiple roles and responsibilities.

Regarding provision for SEN children, the expectation is that their learning needs will be met at the Early Years School Action and Early Years Action Plus phases of SEN provision. However, some children with learning and/or behavioural difficulties that cannot be accommodated at the Action phases, may require learning support obtained through a statutory assessment and a statement of SEN. In this legislative context, class-room staff are required to work with outside agencies and a wide range of professionals, such as educational psychologists, education welfare officers, speech and language thera-pists to provide comprehensive learning and behavioural support services.

The learning and behavioural support services provided for children with SEN are two fold: support to individual pupils, as well as training for school staff with regard to SEN provision. The Education Welfare Officers (EWOs) are primarily responsible for school attendance by working with pupils who have a poor attendance record and their families. The EWOs typically have a good understanding of the family workings and the community context in that they remit also includes child protection. Educational psychologists are involved in assessing children who present learning, social and behavioural/emotional difficulties, and providing advice to teachers and other class-room staff as to how they can best support SEN pupils. Normally this intervention takes place at the School Action Plus stage. Speech and Language Therapists have a long history of working with schools, traditionally, on a 'pull out' capacity by taking a pupil out of the classroom to concentrate on developing specific language skills. Working in partnership with outside agencies at a consultative, organisational or individual level is an new territory where newly qualified teachers and early years practitioners can certainly benefit from support and advice.

## Three-way collaboration: parents, teachers and other professionals

To be effective, as an early years practitioner, you need to build triadic relationships with parents and outside professionals, especially when dealing with children with SEN and other complex needs. This is not always easy, requiring you to develop good communication, negotiation and problem solving skills.

The following is a case study where professionals from different disciplines (e.g. social work, psychology) provide their input for a decision to be made about a SEN statement. This case study illustrates the complexity of the interactions between teachers/classroom staff, parents and outside professionals, and raises issues regarding professionals bound-aries, confidentiality and evidence-based decisions regarding SEN provision. Specifically, this case describes the involvement of a social worker during a statutory assessment, to comment on the family's structures and circumstances as they relate to the child's educational needs. The parents were not satisfied with the assertions made by the social worker in that they felt that her arguments were simplistic and not based on evidence or a thorough understanding of their family situation. Also, the parents felt that the social worker made decisions about their child's educational placement based on a limited information regarding their and their child's functioning. Finally, they felt that the social worker transcended her professional boundaries, stating that

> It is entirely inappropriate for the social worker, while successfully dealing with family issues, and totally ignorant of our child's needs, to make some argument along the lines "he should go to a special school because his mother is depressed and if he goes to a normal school and it doesn't work she might become more depressed".

Moreover, the parents argued that obtaining a SEN statement should not be based on a collection of fragmented pieces of evidence and disparate professional decisions or 'votes', but on integrating multiple pieces of evidence. In this case, there was a clash between the issues raised by the social worker regarding family circumstances, i.e. social isolation, feelings of helplessness, and those concerning the young child's SEN, namely social interaction, restricted use of language as a social tool and behavioural concerns. The father specifically stated

> I am unhappy that a procedure is in place whereby any professional asked for advice for educational statementing should automatically assume they are being asked to make a decision about what sort of educational provision is best. Educational statementing is not a vote, in which each professional votes for his favourite choice of provision.

The parents felt that the social worker's statement about the family's financial situation ('The family's financial resources are being stretched to the limit.') was inappropriate to be included in an educational statement that will be circulated widely among professionals, family friends and neighbours (those who volunteer their services to the village school). The parents argued that other comments that 'would be helpful to the friends and neighbours who will be working with our son, and which might, for instance, welcome them to become involved' should have been included instead.

Finally, the parents stated that the role of child professionals should extend to raise awareness about children's educational and social needs in schools and the immediate community. They also felt that professionals should be active in 'removing blame' placed on parents whose children's difficulties are perceived as resulting from an improper and irresponsible upbringing. In this case, the parents felt that it was not helpful to include statements such as 'It would be debatable as to whether these are due to his diagnosis or his current home circumstances' in the context of an educational evaluation.

This case study illustrates evocatively the importance of taking a multi-disciplinary approach to deciding children's educational provision, keeping open channels of communication with parents to avoid misunderstanding and, being aware of professional boundaries and limitations. Also, issues with regard to ethics (e.g. confidentiality and decisions about disclosure of private information) are raised in the context of dealing with families with SEN children. For practitioners, it involves serious ethical considerations to tease out the pieces of information that are relevant and, thus, appropriate to be disclosed in educational reports, and information that should remain confidential. Making these decisions requires an understanding of children's family practices, values and beliefs, as well as the parents' perspectives about what they consider to be sensitive and relevant information.

## Summary

In this chapter, the roles of teaching and learning assistants and outside professionals and agencies are delineated based on research evidence about good classroom practice. A number of issues regarding parental involvement, collaboration and teamwork are raised, emphasising the diverse perspectives of parents with regard to educational provision. On a positive side, child professionals working together will have the chance to learn from each other and realise that teaching is not a one man/woman act but a team effort. Hopefully, this realisation will make early years practitioners more confident by being part of a community of educators, a cohesive function which is likely to help them test ideas and classroom teaching practices regarding young pupils' learning and development.

# Final thoughts

Early years education is going through an unprecedented upheaval and expansion. Nationally and internationally, there is a growing awareness of the importance of good quality of early years education and care for children's learning and social and emotional development. In many countries, early years education is seen by politicians and policy makers as a platform for social reform, especially for children and their families who experience social and economic disadvantage. In the UK in particular, the government has devoted a considerable political and financial capital to ensure that every child has a good start with education, by maximising places for three-year olds in early years settings.

Approaching early years education as a vehicle for social change is empowering. However, the development of early years education and care as a profession requires re-thinking at macro-level (societal practices, policy) and micro-level (family experiences and influences, understandings of childhood). Social change achieved through early years education should be intrinsically connected to how we view children and ascertain their rights by applying the principles of citizenship and equal opportunities, and how we best educate and cater for them, especially young children who present diverse needs and, possibly, experience social disadvantage.

There is a growing consensus among early years practitioners and policy makers that the scope of early years education should be wider than merely 'delivering' the curriculum and raising standards to embrace pedagogy. This can be achieved by nurturing staff–child interactions and the development of emotional bonds, and taking into account family-based learning and experiences and the wider social and cultural context of children's lives. The Finish Ministry of Education illustrates the importance of a wide scope of early years education by stating that:

> Special attention is given to the need for daycare that implants in the child a sense of social responsibility, understanding the need for peace and concern for the environment.

Social responsibility, social relatedness, empathy, ability to form emotional links with others, language and communication development and a broader understanding of the world and the environment are, undoubtedly, important outcomes of a responsive early years pedagogy. Education and care should be integrated and informed by the principles and knowledge of human development, both sociological and psychological (Gammage, 2003). This is relevant and timely in that, currently, teacher training programmes are characterised by an uneasy separation between psychology/sociology and pedagogy, likely to have a significant impact on early years education and care. With this in mind, in this book, I approached the needs of children with dyslexia from an educational, linguistic and social-emotional perspective, in that I strongly believe that learning, emotional maturity and social adjustment are intertwined and cannot (should not) be separated.

The quality of early years education is the key theme emerging in almost all research studies reviewed in this book. To fulfill the ambition of early years education to promote inclusion by offering children a better start to primary school requires an understanding of what makes early years education effective. As I am writing this book, the results from a large, longitudinal study, the Effective Provision of Pre-School Education (EPPE), revealed, among other things, that good quality of early years education 'irons out' the effects of social and economic disadvantage, and that the quality of interactions between early years staff, children and their parents contributes to the effectiveness of early years education.

Furthermore, other studies reviewed in this book have stressed the importance of emotional attachment, consistency, play and social interaction for linguistic, emotional and social development and learning. Specifically, certain principles that make early years education work have been identified including

- a good quality of the interactions between early years staff, children and their families;
- an understanding of how young children learn by acknowledging their diverse needs;
- a family-centred early years provision by building close relationships with parents based on mutual respect and honesty, and taking into account the home influences on children's learning and development;
- staff qualifications, training opportunities and systems of collegial support;
- an integrated approach towards young children's learning and social and emotional development;
- an understanding of and building upon children's family-based experiences, languages, values and interactional styles that children bring into early years settings;
- the strength of emotional bonds between children and staff to nurture children's natural curiosity, enthusiasm and confidence to develop social and emotional literacy;
- a flexible approach to implementing the curriculum by placing an emphasis on play and activity-orientated learning, and being aware of children's starting point, pace of learning, characteristics and dispositions as learners; and
- a consideration of multiple facets of diversity to 'ensure that all children feel included, secure and valued', especially children with SEN (QCA, 2000: 11).

To summarise these principles, what makes early years education and care effective is a good quality of teaching and learning and, most importantly, an awareness of issues of children's rights and entitlement and children's emotional attachment. For early years practitioners, it is essential to realise the complexity and diversity in children's life, their parents' and that of the surrounding community, as well as the changing nature of childhood. There is a continuous change in our understanding of how young children learn changes continously; however, it is widely accepted that language, social-emotional development and a desire to learn flourish in the context of intimate, three-way relationships between children, their teachers and caregivers/parents.

A unique feature of early years education is its closeness with children's family. Clearly, good home–school relationships are important throughout primary and secondary schooling. For early years education, in particular, recognising the structures, values and social and cultural dynamics of children's family has important implications for mapping the developmental and learning needs of young children and re-assessing the less clear-cut boundaries between typical and atypical development. Early years education and care should be placed on a continuum of provision across family, daycare/nursery, and pre-school settings, making parental involvement and collaborative workings between staff and parents the main drive.

The role of early years staff is seen as pivotal in supporting children to make a good start and achieve academically. Early years staff's responsibilities are constantly expanding, being required to 'invest' in children and develop good practice, and become what Gammage describes 'carers of vision and compassion' to undertake the demands of combining education and care (2003: 1). In the current climate of financial constraints, early years profession's reduced status, heavy workloads and lack of employment stability, maintaining high quality of early years provision are serious challenges for early years staff and policy makers alike.

This book recognises the need to provide early years practitioners with an understanding of children's development and learning grounded on research and examples of good practice. It also recognises the rewards and challenges that practitioners face to help children make a good start with their schooling. Some of the topics discussed in this book revolve around ways of supporting early years staff to undertake the enormous challenge of providing for all young children, especially those with dyslexia. The main aim of the guidance on classroom practice provided in this book is to stimulate you, as a practitioner, to engage in a critical appraisal of what works and what does not, and understand how the social and political reality influences children's lives.

I hope that this book will contribute, albeit in a minor way, towards educating rather than merely training you as an early years practitioner. The challenge for you is to go beyond child minding and become reflective on and aware of issues and understandings of childhood and, hopefully, fascinated by the diversity inherent in human development.

# Useful web addresses

The British Dyslexia Association, 98 London Road, Reading, Berkshire, RG1 5AU. The website is http://www.bda-dyslexia.org.uk

The National Association for Special Educational Needs (NASEN), York House, Exhall Grange, Wheelwright Lane, Coventry, CV7 9HP. The website is www.nasen.org.uk. This website is for educational professionals and provides information about teaching and learning resources and material, as well as classroom management. The Royal College of Speech and Language Therapists. The Web address is http://www.rcslt.org.

This is the website, http://www.bda.org.uk, for the British Dyslexia Association for information and advice on issues regarding assessment and identification of dyslexia, as well as teaching methods and strategies targeting dyslexia-associated difficulties.

This is the web address, http://www.qca.org.uk, for the Qualifications and Curriculum Authority. You can easily download a very useful document, published by the DfES, titled 'Curriculum Guidance for the Foundation Stage'.

The website for the National Grid for Learning (www.ngfl.gov.uk) is a gateway for educational resources that teachers can access to facilitate their teaching.

Information about visual strain and the use of tinted overlays and glasses to support reading may be obtained from the *Colour and Visual Sensitivity Information Group* at the University of Essex. The web address is http://www.essex.ac.uk/psychology/overlays

Also, the Dyslexia Research Trust, at Magdalen College of the University of Oxford, is a good source of information about visual perceptual difficulties as they relate to dyslexia.

If you would like to obtain detailed information about young children's demonstrable behaviours with regard to literacy, language and social-emotional development, you can access a chapter titled 'Access to the Foundation Stage Profile for Children with a range of Special Needs at the Foundation Stage' published by the DfES. The web address is http://www.standards. dfes.gov.uk/parentalinvolvement

Also, information about teaching practices and initiatives can be obtained from http://www.teachernet.gov.uk/professionaldevelopment/managingmycdp/teachingassistants.

## ICT Resources

The following resources are for Learning Support Assistants that run Early Literacy Support (ELS) intervention sessions. It is an essential guide to run daily sessions including details to help you prepare sessions as well as a full script. The ELS programmes materials can be obtained electronically by visiting the web page: http://www.teachernet.gov.uk. From there, you will be able to download ELS activity sheets for parents and caregivers, ELS sessions for 12 weeks and photocopy material. Access to these materials can also be requested by sending an email to dfes@prolog.uk.com

There is a plethora of information that can be downloaded from the web page of DfES Publications, http://www.standards.dfes.gov.uk/literacy/publications.

A very good guide for ICT resources for children with dyslexia is the Computer Users' Bulletin that is published by the Computer Working Party of the British Dyslexia Association. Also, Becta is a great source for information about software for pupils and suggestions and teaching practices for teachers (http://www.becta.org.uk).

Suppliers for the software programmes listed in Chapter 6 are:

- Rickitt Educational Media (REM), Software Directory, Great Western House, Langport, Somerset, TA10 9YU.
- Listen, Think and Do: This is for Reception, Year 1 and 2 pupils targeting reading and listening skills.
- GAMZ Player CD.
- Mastering Memory.

More information about software programmes tailored for children with SEN can be obtained from the website http://www.inclusive.co.uk

The BBC Education website (http://www.bbc.co.uk/education/schools) offers online resources/documents that can be downloaded easily. You can access resources to support phonological development, reading and writing in children for all ages.

Listening Books (The National Listening Library), 12 Lant Street, London, SE1 1QH.

The following is a collection of websites for activities related to maths and nature for young children.

- maths – http://www.ambleside.school.co.uk/ambleweb/mentalmaths
- nature – http://naturegrid.org.uk/infant

The following information was obtained from the Early Years Online website managed by Learning and Teaching Scotland. The main address for this website is http://www.itscotland.org.uk/earlyyears/ICTstrategy.asp

*Aesthetic development*
http://www.artcyclopedia.com/
In this website, there are links to national and international galleries. A wide range of artworks can be searched by artist name, art movement, subject, artist's nationality or medium.

http://www.bgfl.org/bgfl14.cfm
This website contains activities to support learning in a range of subject areas for children aged five to eight.

http://www.earlybirdsmusic.com/songs.html
This site contains a wide selection of downloadable songs for early years. The songs are accompanied by words and animated actions.

http://www.geocities.com/EnchantedForest/5329/2index.html
This web site has a large selection of music files that can be shared with children. Categories of music include children's songs, Christmas songs, national anthems and classical pieces. It offers an entertaining way to introduce children to music.

http://www.channel4.com/learning/microsites/H/hoobs/activities/
These activities allow children to create unique images by selecting different elements from a number of possible choices.

http://www.channel4.com/learning/microsites/H/hoobs/activities/
Children can 'paint' pictures of the Hoobs by using the mouse to select different paint colours that can be used to fill areas of an image with colour. There are also opportunities to see which colours are created when two colours are mixed. Children can compose their own drag-and-drop images of space and seaside scenes.

http://www.bbc.co.uk/schools/laac/music/fdi.html
This site has interactive music activities that require children to listen to and repeat patterns of sounds.

*Communication and language*
http://www.bgfl.org/bgfl/4.cfm
This website contains activities to support learning in a range of subject areas for children aged five to eight.

http://teacher.scholastic.com/clifford1/flash/phonics/index.htm
Children are presented with a selection of images and asked to find the words which begin with the same sound as a main picture. The names of pictures are said out loud when clicked.

http://www.bbc.co.uk/cbeebies/funandgames/
This educational website contains a selection of online activities and includes well-known characters from BBC programmes. Activities involve recognising letters, matching letters and selecting consonants for use at the beginning of tree letter words.

http://www.enchantedlearning.com/Dictionary.html
This site offers an online picture dictionary, which contains a range of images for each letter of the alphabet. This site could be presented on an interactive whiteboard as part of a phonics lesson. There are options to look at words in different languages, including French, German, Spanish and Italian.

http://www.itscotland.com/storybook/
This site is an interactive resource to help children and teachers explore language and creative writing. Eight books are presented along with related games, word banks and interviews with authors.

http://www.bbc.co.uk/schools/
This site has a selection of animated stories with audio support.

http://www.seussville.com/seussville/
This animated website contains interactive activities related to the Dr Seuss stories. Games include opportunities to use positional language.

*Emotional, personal and social development*
http://www.assemblies.org.uk
This site provides background information and activities for assemblies. Religious festivals and events within the life of the school are covered in detail.

*Environment and maths*
http://www.abc.net.au/dinosaurs/dino_playground/default.htm
This educational website contains a number of games and puzzles suitable for young children. Examples of games, which all follow a dinosaur theme, include memory match, online jigsaws, sliding puzzles, video clips and images. There is also an opportunity to find out more about individual dinosaurs and to look at dinosaur bones and think about where particular parts of the skeleton are located.

http://www.bbc.co.uk/education/dynamo/lab/index.shtml
This website contains interactive activities that involve recognising the difference between living things and non-living things and also recognising the difference between plants and animals in their environments.

http://www.kidspsych.org/oochy.html
Online games for young children aiming at developing cognitive thinking skills and deductive reasoning in a fun context. Games involve matching shapes, navigating through a maze and develop awareness of cause and effect. Each activity has notes for adults to explain the purpose of the activity and suggest further reading.

http://perso.wanadoo.fr/jeux.lulu/english.htm
This site includes a range of interactive maths activities for young children. These include activities to develop logic, number skills and memory. The activities may be most appropriate for use with small groups with adult support.

http://www.bbc.co.uk/schools/numbertime/index.shtml
This website contains activities to support teaching and learning of mathematical concepts in early years. It provides games, songs, animations and ideas. Based on the popular series BBC Numbertime, it includes areas such as recognising numbers, counting on, addition, subtraction and number sequences.

http://www.channel4.com/learning/microsites/H/hoobs/activities.
A selection of activities that ask children to match objects, colours, shapes or silhouettes in a selection of different games contexts.

http://www.channel4.com/learning/microsites/H/hoobs/activities/
Activities that involve recognising letters, matching letters and selecting consonants for use at the beginning of tree letter words. Familiar Hoobs characters are a part of each game.

http://www.channel4.com/learning/microsites/H/hoobs/activities
In these games children are presented with four pictures and have to decide which is the odd one out. For example, fish, dog, cat, rabbit – which is the odd one out? These activities are challenging and could be used to provoke interesting discussion amongst children.

# References

Adams, M.J. (1990) *Beginning to Read. Children Thinking and Learning About Print*, Cambridge, MA: MIT Press.

Alder, C. and Sandor, D. (1990) 'Youth researching youth', *Youth Studies*, 9(4): 38–42.

Allen, D.M. and Tarnowski, K.J. (1989) 'Depressive characteristics of physically abused children', *Journal of Abnormal Psychology*, 71(1): 1–11.

Anderson, V. (1992) 'A teacher development project in transactional strategy instruction for teachers of severely reading-disabled adolescents', *Teaching and Teacher Education*, 8: 391–403.

Anning, A. and Edwards, A. (1999) *Promoting Children's Language from Birth to Five. Developing the New Early Years Professional*, Buckingham: Open University Press.

Aram, D. and Hall, N. (1989) 'Longitudinal follow-up of communication pre-school disorders: treatment implications', *School Psychological Review*, 18: 487–501.

Au, K.H. (1992) 'Constructing the theme of a story', *Language Arts*, 69: 106–111.

Au, K.H. and Kawakami, A.J. (1994) 'Cultural congruence in instruction', in E.R. Hollins, J.E. King and W. Hayman (eds.), *Teaching Diverse Populations: Formulating a Knowledge Base*, Albany, NY: State University of New York Press.

Aubrey, C. (2004) 'Implementing the Foundation Stage in reception classes', *British Educational Research Journal*, 30(5): 633–656.

Aubrey, C., David, T., Godfrey, R. and Thompson, L. (2000) *Early Childhood Educational Research: Issues in Methodology and Ethics*, London and New York: Routledge and Farmer.

Audet, L. and Tankersley, M. (1999) 'Use of self-talk strategies to enhance comprehension and behaviour', Poster session presented at annual American Speech-Language-Hearing Association convention, Boston, MA.

Baker, L. and Cantwell, D. (1991) *Psychiatric and Developmental Disorders in Children with Communication Disorders*, Washington, DC: American Psychological Press.

Barkley, R.A. (1990) *Attention Deficit Hyperactivity Disorder: A Handbook for Diagnosis and Treatment*, Guilford Press: New York.

Baron-Cohen, S. (1995) *Mindblindness*, Cambridge, MA: MIT Press.

Basic Skills Agency (2003) *Young Children's Skills on Entry to Education*, London: Basic Skills Agency.

Becker, J.M. (1996) *Peer Coaching for Improvement of Teaching and Learning Teachers*. Network. Online. Available HTTP: <http://www.teachnet.org/TNPI/research/growth/becker.htm.> (Accessed 12 February 2003).

Becta (2004) *A Review of the Research Literature on Barriers to the Uptake of ICT by Teachers*. British Educational Communication Technology Agency. Online. Available HTTP: <http://www.becta.org.uk/page_documents/research/barriers.pdf> (Accessed November 2004).

Bennett, N., Wood, E. and Rogers, S. (1997) *Teaching Through Play: Teachers' Thinking and Classroom Practice*, Buckingham: Open University Press.

Bills, L. (2004) 'Working with parents and other adults', in V. Brooks, I. Abbott and Liz Bills (eds.) *Preparing to Teach in Secondary Schools*, McGraw-Hill: Open University Press.

Bills, L. and Brooks, V. (2004) 'Using differentiation to support learning' in V. Brooks, I. Abbott and Liz Bills (eds.) *Preparing to Teach in Secondary Schools*, McGraw-Hill: Open University Press.

Booth, T., Ainscow, M., Black-Hawkins, K., Vaughan, M. and Shaw, L. (2000) *Index for Inclusion: Developing Learning and Participation in Schools*, Bristol: CSIE.

Boudreau, D.M. and Hedberg, N.L. (1999) 'A comparison of early literacy skills in children with specific language impairment and their typically developing peers', *American Journal of Speech-Language Pathology*, 8: 249–60.

Bourdieu, P. (1973) 'Cultural reproduction and social reproduction', in R. Brown (ed.) *Knowledge, Education and Cultural Change*, London: Tavistock Publications.

British Psychological Society (BPS) (1999) *Dyslexia, Literacy and Psychological Assessment*, Leicester: British Psychological Society.

Brooker, L. and Siraj-Blatchford, J. (2002). ' "Click on Miaow!": how children of three and four years experience the nursery computer', *Contemporary Issues in Early Childhood*, 3(2): 251–273.

Browne, A. (1998) 'Provision for reading for four year old children', *Reading*, 32(1): 9–13.

Caldarella, P. and Merrell, K.W. (1997) 'Common dimensions of social skills of children and adolescents: a taxonomy of positive behaviours', *School Psychology Review*, 26(2): 264–278.

Carr, M. and May, H. (2000) 'TeWhariki: curriculum voices', in H. Penn (ed.) *Early Childhood Services: Theory, Policy and Practice*, Buckingham: Open University Press.

Carriedo, N. and Alonso-Tapia, J. (1996) 'Main idea comprehension: training teachers and effects on students', *Journal of Research in Reading*, 19: 111–127.

Carvel, C. (1999) 'Play is out, early learning is in', *The Guardian*, 23 June.

Catts, H.W. and Hugh, W. (1996) 'Defining dyslexia as a developmental language disorder. An expanded view', *Topics in Language Disorders*, 16(2): 14–29.

Catts, H.W. and Kamhi, A.G. (eds.) (1999) *Language and Reading Disabilities*, Boston, MA: Allyn & Bacon.

Chan, L. (1996) 'Combined strategy and attributional training for seventh grade average and poor readers', *Journal of Research in Reading*, 19: 111–127.

Chaney, C. (1992) 'Language development, metalinguistic skills, and print awareness in 3-year-old children', *Applied Psycholinguistics*, 13: 485–514.

Cline, T. (1992) 'Assessment of special educational needs: meeting reasonable expectations?' in T. Cline (ed.) *The Assessment of Special Educational Needs: International Perspectives*, London: Routledge.

Cline, T. and Shamsi, T. (2000). *Language Needs or Special Needs? The Assessment of Learning Difficulties in Literacy Among Children Learning English as an Additional Language: A Literature Review*. London: DfEE.

Cooke, A. (2002) *Tackling Dyslexia* (second edition), London: Whurr Publishers.

Cuban, L. (1999) The technology puzzle. *Education Week*, 18(43). Online. Available HTTP: <http://www.edweek.org/ew/vol-18/43cuban.h18> (Accessed November 2004).

Cummins, J. (1984) *Bilinguism and Special Education: Issues in Assessment and Pedagogy*, Clevedon: Multilingual Matters.

Cunningham, C. and Davis, H. (1985) *Working with Parents. Frameworks for Collaboration*, Milton Keynes: Open University Press.

Dale, P.S., Crain-Thoreson, C., Notari-Syverson, A. and Cole, K. (1996) 'Parent–child book reading as an intervention for young children with language delays', *Topics in Early Childhood Special Education*, 16: 213–35.

Dawes, L. (2000) 'The National Grid for Learning and the professional development of teachers: outcomes of an opportunity for dialogue', Unpublished PhD thesis.

De Lemos, M. (2002) *Closing the Gap Between Research and Practice: Foundations for the Acquisition of Literacy*. Camberwell, Victoria: Australian Centre for Educational Research.

Denckla, M.B. and Rudel, R.G. (1976) 'Rapid Automatized Naming (RAN): Dyslexia differentiated from other learning disabilities', *Neuropsychologia*, 14: 474–479.

Department of Education and Employment (DfEE) (1996) *Education Act*, London: DfEE Publications.

Department for Education and Employment (DfEE) (1998) *The National Literacy Strategy Framework for Teaching*, London: DfEE Publications.

Department for Education and Employment (DfEE/QCA) (2000) *Curriculum Guidance for the Foundation Stage*, London: QCA.

Department of Education and Science (DES) (1978) *Special Educational Need (Report of the Warnock Committee)*, London: HMSO.

Department for Education and Skills (DfES) (2001) *Special Education Needs Code of Practice*, London: DfES.

Department for Education and Skills (DfES) (2002) *Extending Opportunities: Raising Standards*, London: DfES.

Dockrell, J.E. and Lindsay, G. (2001) 'Children with specific speech and language difficulties – the teachers' perspective', *Oxford Review of Education*, 27: 369–394.

Dowling, M. (2001) *Young Children's Personal, Social and Emotional Development*, London: Paul Chapman.

Duck, S. (1991) *Friends for Life. The Psychology of Personal Relationships* (2nd edition), Hemel Hempstead: Harvester/Wheatsheaf.

Dunn, J. (1993) *Young Children's Close Relationships: Beyond Attachment*, London: Sage.

Early Years Curriculum Group (1989) *First Things First: Educating Young Children*, Oldham, England: Madeleine Lindley.

Ertmer, P., Addison, P., Lane, M., Ross, E. and Woods, D. (1999) 'Examining Teachers' Beliefs about the Role of Technology in the Elementary Classroom', *Journal of Research on Computing in Education*, 32(1): 54–72.

Ezell, H., Justice, L. and Parsons, D. (2000) 'Enhancing the emergent literacy skills of pre-schoolers with communication disorders: a pilot investigation', *Child Language Teaching and Therapy*, 16(2): 121–140.

Fawcett, A.J. and Nicolson, R.I. (1999) 'Performance of dyslexic children on cognitive and cerebellar tests', *Journal of Motor Behavior*, 31: 68–79.

Florian, L. (2004) 'Uses of technology that support pupils with special educational needs', in L. Florian and S. Hegarty (eds.), *ICT and Special Educational Needs. A Tool for Inclusion*, McGraw-Hill: Open University Press.

Frederickson, N., Frith, U. and Reason, R. (1997) *Phonological Assessment Battery*, Windsor: NFER-Nelson.

Frederickson, N. and Frith, U. (1998) 'Identifying Dyslexia in bilingual children: a phonological approach with Inner London Sylheti speakers', *Dyslexia*, 4: 119–131.

Frederickson, N. and Cline, T. (2002) *Special Educational Needs, Inclusion and Diversity. A textbook*, Buckingham: Open University Press.

Gammage, P. (2003) 'The Sacred and the profane in early childhood: An Englishman's view', *Contemporary Issues in Early Childhood*, 4(3): 34–56.

Gathercole, S.E. and Baddeley, A.D. (1989) 'Evaluation of the role of phonological STM in the development of vocabulary in children: A longitudinal study', *Journal of Memory and Language*, 28: 200–213.

Goldschmied, E. and Jackson, S. (1996) *People Under Three*, London: Routledge.

Goleman, D. (1995) *Emotional Intelligence*, New York: Bantam.

Green, J.L., Weade, R. and Graham, K. (1988) 'Lesson construction and student participation: A sociolinguistic analysis', in J.L. Green and J.O. Harker (eds.), *Multiple Perspective Analysis of Classroom Discourse*, Norwood, NJ: Ablex.

Gross, J. (2002) *Special Educational Needs in the Primary School: A Practical Guide* (3rd edition), Buckingham, MK: Open University Press.

Guha, S. (2000) *Are we all technically prepared? Teachers' perspectives on the causes of comfort or discomfort in using computers at elementary grade teaching.* Paper presented at the Annual Meeting of the National Association for the Education of Young Children Atlanta, GA, 8–11 November 2000.

Hartas, D. (2004) 'Teacher and Speech/Language Therapist Collaboration: Being equal and achieving a common goal?', *Child Language Teaching and Therapy*, 20(1): 33–54.

Hartas, D. (2005) *Language and Communication Difficulties*, London: Continuum.

Hartas, D. and Donahue, M. (1996) 'Conversational and social problem solving skills in adolescents with learning disabilities', *Learning Disability Research and Practice*, 12(4): 213–220.

Hartas, D. and Patrikakou, E. (1997) 'Friendship and conversational skills in adolescents with behavioural or emotional disorders', *British Columbia Journal of Special Education*, 21(2): 5–32.

Hartas, D. and Warner, B.J. (2000) 'A form of dyslexia? Pupils with language and reading difficulties', *Educational Psychology in Practice*, 15(4): 246–255.

Hargreaves, D.H. (1996) *Teaching as Research-based Profession: Possibilities and Prospects*, Teacher Training Agency Annual Lecture, London: Teacher Training Agency.

Harker, J.O. (1988) 'Contrasting the content of two story-reading lessons: A propositional analysis', in J.L. Green and J.O. Harker (eds.) *Multiple Perspective Analyses of Classroom Discourse, Vol. 28, Advances in Discourse Processes*, Norwood, NJ: Ablex.

Henderson, A.T. and Berla, N. (eds.) (1994) *A New Generation of Evidence: The Family is Critical to Student Achievement*, Washington, DC: Center for Law and Education.

Hewitt, L.E. and Duchan, J.F. (1995) 'Subjectivity in children's fictional narrative', *Topics in Language Disorders*, 15(4): 1–15.

Hockenberger, E.H., Goldstein, H. and Haas, L.S. (1999) 'Effects of commenting by mothers with low socioeconomic status during joint bookreading', *Topics in Early Childhood Special Education*, 19: 15–27.

Hornberger, N.H. (1992) 'Biliteracy contexts, continua, and contrasts: Policy and curriculum for Cambodian and Puerto Rican students in Philadelphia', *Education and Urban Society*, 24(2): 196–211.

Gillam, R.B. and Johnston, J.R. (1985) 'Development of print awareness in language-disordered pre-schoolers', *Journal of Speech and Hearing Research*, 28: 521–26.

Jacques, M. (2004) 'The Death of Intimacy', *The Guardian*, 18 September.

Jarvis, J. and Lamb, S. (2001) 'Interaction and the development of communication in the under twos: issues for practitioners working with young children', *Early Education*, 21(2): 129–138.

Kendall, P.C., Stark, K.D. and Adam, T. (1990), 'Cognitive deficit or cognitive distortion of childhood depression', *Journal of Abnormal Psychology*, 18: 255–270.

Killion, J.P. (1990) 'The benefits of an induction program for experienced teachers', *Journal of Staff Development*, 11(4): 32–36.

Klug, B.J. and Salzman, S.A. (1991) 'Formal induction vs. informal mentoring: Comparative effects and outcomes', *Teaching and Teacher Education*, 7: 241–251.

Laevers, F. and Van Sanden, P. (1995) *Basic Book for Experiential Pre-Primary Education*, Leuven, Belgium: Centre for Experiential Education.

Lang, P. (1998) 'Getting round to clarity: what do we mean by Circle-Time?', *Pastoral Care in Education*, 16(3): 3–10.

Lapp, D. and Flood, J. (1986) *Teaching Students to Read*, New York: Macmillan Publishing Company.

Lawrence, D. (1996) *Enhancing Self Esteem in the Classroom* (2nd edition), London: Paul Chapman Publishers.

Lee, D. (1997) 'Factors influencing the success of computer skills learning among in-service teachers', *British Journal of Educational Technology*, 28(2): 139–141.

Lindsay, G. (2004) 'Baseline assessment and the early identification of dyslexia', in G. Reid and A. Fawcett (eds.) *Dyslexia in Context: Research, Policy and Practice*, London: Whurr.

Lloyd, C. (2002) 'Developing and changing practice in special educational needs through critically reflective action research: a case study', *European Journal of Special Needs Education*, 17(2): 109–127.

Lovegrove, W.J., Garzia, R.P. and Nicholson, S.B. (1990) 'Experimental evidence of a transient system deficit in specific reading disability', *Journal of the American Optometric Association*, 61: 137–146.

Lou, Y., Abrami, P.C. and d'Apollonia, S. (2001) 'Small group and individual learning with technology: a meta-analysis', *Review of Educational Research*, 71(3): 449–521.

McBride, B.A., Rane, T.R. and Bae, J.H. (2001) 'Intervening with teachers to encourage father male involvement in early childhood programs', *Early Childhood Research Quarterly*, 16(1): 77–93.

McCulloch, G., Helsby, G. and Knight, P. (2000) *The Politics of Professionalism*, London: Continuum.

Menter, I., Muschamp, P., Nicholls, P., Ozga, J. and Pollard, A. (1997) *Work and Identity in the Primary School*, Philadelphia: Open University Press.

Miller, L. (2000) 'Play as a foundation for learning', in R. Drury, L. Miller and R. Campbell (eds.) *Looking at Early Years Education and Care*, London: David Fulton.

Miles, E. (1989) *The Bangor Dyslexia Teaching System*, London: Whurr.

Mosley, J. (1996) *Quality Circle Time in the Primary Classroom*, Volume 1. LDA.

Mosley, J. and Tew, M. (1999) *Quality Circle Time in the Secondary Schools: A Handbook of Good Practice*, London: David Fulton.

Moss, P. and Petrie, P. (2002) *From Children's Services to Children's Spaces*, London: RoutledgeFalmer.

Moyles, J. (2001) 'Passion, Paradox and Professionalism in Early Years Education', *Early Years: Journal of International Research and Development*, 21(2): 81–95.

Moyles, J., Adams, S. and Musgrave, A. (2002) *Study of Pedagogical Effectiveness in Early Learning (SPEEL)*, London: Department for Education and Skills.

National Commission on Teaching and America's Future (September 1996) *What Matters Most: Teaching for America's Future*. Online. Available HTTP: <http://www.tc.columbia.edu/~teachcomm/WhatMattersMost.pdf.> (Accessed 2 April 2003).

National Primary Strategy (2003) *Excellence and Enjoyment: A Strategy for Primary Schools*, London: DfES Publication.

National Staff Development Council (2001) *NSDC Standards for Staff Development. Online.* Available HTTP: <http://www.nsdc.org/library/standards2001.html.> (Accessed 6 April 2004).

Nicholas, H. (1991) 'Language awareness and second language development', in C. James and P. Garrett (eds.) *Language Awareness in the Classroom*, London: Longman.

Nicolson, R.I. (1999) 'Reading, skill and dyslexia', in D. Messer and S. Millar (eds.), *Exploring Developmental Psychology*, London: Arnold.

Nicolson, R. and Fawcett, A. (2000) 'Long-term learning in dyslexic children', *European Journal of Cognitive Psychology*, 12(3): 357–393.

Oakhill, J. and Garnham, A. (1989) *Becoming a Skilled Reader*, Oxford: Basil Blackwell.

Oden, S. (1986) 'A child's social isolation: origins, prevention, intervention', in G. Cartledge and J.F. Milburn (eds.), *Teaching Social Skills to Children*, Oxford: Pergamon Press.

Organisation for Economic Cooperation and Development (OECD) (2001a) *Starting Strong. Early Childhood Education and Care*, Paris: OECD.

Orlik, S. (2004) 'The professional framework and professional values and practice', in V. Brooks, I. Abbott and Liz Bills (eds.) *Preparing to Teach in Secondary Schools*, McGraw-Hill: Open University Press.

Pang, E. and Kamil, M. (2004) *Second Language Issues in Early Literacy and Instruction*, Stanford University, CA: Publication Series No. 1.

Parke, T. and Drury, R. (2001) 'Language development at home and school: gains and losses in young bilinguals', *Early Years*, 21(2): 117–127.

Pearl, R., Bryan, T. and Donahue, M. (1980) 'Learning disabled children's attributions for success and failure', *Learning Disability Quarterly*, 3: 3–9.

Pershey, M. (2000) 'Children's elicited use of pragmatic language functions: how six- and seven-year-old children adapt to the interactional environments of story scenarios', *Language Awareness*, 9(4): 218–235.

Piotrowski, J. and Reason, R (2000) 'The National Literacy Strategy and dyslexia: a comparison of teaching methods and materials', *Support for Learning*, 15(2): 51–67.

Pollard, A. and Filer, A. (eds) (1999) *The Social World of Children's Careers: Strategic Biographies Through Primary School*, London: Cassell.

Prizant, B.M. (1999) 'Early intervention: young children with communication and emotional/ behavioural problems', in D. Rogers-Adkinson and P. Griffith (eds.), *Communication Disorders and Children with Psychiatric and Behavioural Disorders*, San Diego: Singular Publishing Group.

Prizant, B.M. and Wetherby, A.M. (1990) 'Toward an integrated view of early language and communication development and socioemotional development', *Topics in Language Disorders*, 10: 1–16.

Pugh, G. (1988) *Services for Under Fives: Developing a Co-ordinated Approach*, London: National Children's Bureau.

Puttalaz, M. and Gottman, J.M. (1981) 'An interactional model of children's entry into peer groups', *Child Development*, 52(3): 986–994.

Qualifications and Curriculum Authority (QCA) (1999) *Early Learning Goals*, DfES/QCA Publications.

Qualifications and Curriculum Authority (2000) *Curriculum Guidance for the Foundation Stage*, London: DfEE Publications.

Qualifications and Curriculum Authority (QCA) (2003) Foundation Stage Profile Handbook, Suffolk: DfES/QCA Publications.

Rack, J.P. (1994) 'Dyslexia: The phonological deficit hypothesis', in A.J. Fawcett and R.I. Nicolson (eds.) *Dyslexia in Children: Multidisciplinary Perspectives*, Hemel Hempstead: Harvester Press.

Ramirez, J.D. (1991) *Executive summary of the final report: longitudinal study of structured English immersion strategy, early exit and late-exit transitional bilingual education programs and language minority children*, San Mateo, CA: Aguirre International.

Raphael, T.E. and McMahon, S.I. (1994) 'Book Club: An alternative framework for reading instruction', *Reading Teacher*, 48: 102–116.

Reason, R. (2001) 'Educational practice and dyslexia', *The Psychologist*, 14(6): 298–300.

Reed, D.S. and McNergney, R.F. (2000) *Evaluating Technology-based Curriculum Materials*, ERIC Digest EDO-SP-2000-5, Washington, DC: ERIC Clearinghouse on Teaching and Teacher Education.

Reich, L.R. (1994) 'Circle time in pre-school: an analysis of educational praxis', *European Early Childhood Education Research Journal*, 2(1): 51–59.

Roffey, S., Tarrant, T. and Majors, K. (1994) *Young Friends: Schools and Friendships*, London: Cassell.

Rosaldo, R. (1993) *Culture and Truth: The Remaking of Social Analysis*, London: Routledge.

Rice, M. (1993). ' "Don't talk to him; he's weird". A social consequences account of language and social interactions', in A.P. Kaiser and D.B. Gray (eds.) *Enhancing Children's Communication: Research Foundations for Intervention*, Baltimore: Paul H. Brookes.

Riddell, S., Wilson, A., Adler, M. and Mordau (2002) 'Parents, professionals and special educational needs policy frameworks in England and Scotland', *Policy and Politics*, 30(3): 411–425.

Riley, J. (ed.) (2003) *Learning in the Early Years: A Guide for Teachers of Children 3–7*, London: Paul Chapman Publishing.

Riley, J., Burrell, A. and McCallum, B. (2004) 'Developing the spoken language skills of reception class children in two multi-cultural, inner-city primary schools', *British Educational Research Journal*, 30(5): 657–672.

Rogers, S. (1991) 'Observation of emotional functioning in young handicapped children', *Child: Care, Health and Development*, 17: 303–312.

Rudel, R.G. (1985) 'The definition of dyslexia: Language and motor deficits', in F.H. Duoey and N. Geschwind (eds.) *Dyslexia: A Neuroscientific Approach to Clinical Evaluation*, Boston: Little Brown.

Russell, G. and Bradley, G. (1997) 'Teachers' computer anxiety: implications for professional development', *Education and Information Technologies*, 2(1): 17–30.

Sabornie, E.J. (1991) 'Measuring and teaching social skills in the mainstream', in G. Stoner, M.R. Shinn and H.M. Walker (eds.) *Interventions for Achievement and Behavior Problems*, Washington, DC: National Association of School Psychologists.

Sammons, P., Elliot, K., Sylva, K., Melhuish, E., Siraj-Blatchford, I. and Taggard, B. (2004) 'The impact of pre-school on young children's cognitive attainments of entry to reception', *British Educational Research Journal*, 30(5): 691–707.

School Curriculum Assessment Authority (SCAA) (1996) *Nursery Education: Desirable Outcomes for Children's Learning on Entering Compulsory Education*, London: SCAA and Department for Education and Employment.

Scrimshaw, P. (2004) *Enabling Teachers to Make Successful Use of ICT*. Becta. Online. Available HTTP: http://www.becta.org.uk/page_documents/research/enablers.pdf (Accesses January 2005).

Searcy, S. and Meadows, N.B. (1994) 'The impact of social structures on friendship development for children with behavioural problems', *Education and Treatment of Children*, 17: 255–266.

Seligman, M.E.P., Peterson, C., Kaslow, N.J., Tanenbaum, R.L., Alloy, L. and Abramson, L.Y. (1984) 'Explanatory style and depressive symptoms among children', *Journal of Abnormal Psychology*, 93: 235–238.

Showers, J. and Joyce, B. (1996) 'The evolution of peer coaching', *Educational Leadership*, 53(6): 12–16.

Shulman, L. (1987) 'Knowledge and teaching: Foundations of the new reform', *Harvard Educational Review*, 63: 161–182.

Siegel, L.S. (1990) 'IQ and learning disabilities: RIP', in H.L. Swanson and B. Keogh (eds.) *Learning Disabilities: Theoretical and Research Issues*, Hillsdale, NJ: Lawrence Erlbaum Associates.

Singh, N.N., Deitz, D.E.D. and Singh, J. (1992) 'Behavioural approaches', in N. Singh and I.L. Beale (eds.) *Learning Disabilities: Nature, Theory, and Treatment*. New York: Springer-Verlag.

Siraj-Blatchford, I., Sulva, K., Muttock, S., Gilden, R. and Bell, D. (2002) *Researching Effective Pedagogy in Early Years*, London: DfES Publications.

Smith, N. (2002) 'Transition to the school playground: an intervention programme for nursery children', *Early Years*, 22(2): 129–146.

Snoeyink, R. and Ertmer, P. (2001) 'Thrust into technology: how veteran teachers respond', *Journal of Educational Technology Systems*, 30(1): 85–111.

Snow, C., Burns, M.S. and Griffin, P. (1998) *Preventing Reading Difficulties in Young Children*, Washington, DC: National Academy Press.

Snowling, M. (1995) 'Phonological processing and developmental dyslexia', *Journal of Research in Reading*, 18: 132–138.

Stanovich, K.E. (1988) 'The right and wrong places to look for the cognitive locus of reading disability', *Annals of Dyslexia*, 38: 154–177.

Stanovich, K.E. (1996) 'Towards a more inclusive definition of dyslexia', *Dyslexia*, 2(3): 154–166.

Stein, J. (1989) 'Visuospatial perception and reading problems', *Irish Journal of Psychology*, 10: 521–533.

Stevens, C. (2004) 'Information and communication technology, special educational needs, and schools: A historical perspective of UK government initiatives', in L. Florian and J. Hegarty (eds.) *ICT and Special Educational Needs: A Tool for Inclusion*, Berkshire: Open University Press.

Strandell, H. (2000) 'What is the use of children's play: Preparation or social participation?' in H. Penn (ed.) *Early Childhood Services, Theory, Policy and Practice*, Buckingham: Open University Press.

Stringer, R. and Stanovich, K. (2000) 'The connection between reaction time and variation in reading ability: Unravelling covariance relationships with cognitive ability and phonological sensitivity', *Scientific Studies of Reading*, 4: 41–53.

Sulzby, E. (1990) 'Assessment of writing and children's language while writing', in L. Mandel-Morrow and J.K. Smith (eds.) *Assessment for Instruction in Early Literacy*, New Jersey: Prentice-Hall.

Thomas, G. (1997) 'Inclusive schools for an inclusive society', *British Journal of Special Education*, 24(3): 103–107.

Walberg, H.J. (1984) 'Improving the productivity of America's schools', *Educational Leadership* (Alexandria, VA), 41(8): 19–27.

Wang, M.C., Haertel, G.D. and Walberg, H.J. (1993a) 'Toward a knowledge base for school learning', *Review of Educational Research* (Washington, DC), 63: 249–94.

Webb, J.T. and Kleine, P.A. (1993) 'Assessing gifted and talented children', in J. Culbertson and D. Willis (eds.), *Testing Young Children*, Austin, TX: Pro-Ed.

Webb, J.T. (1993) 'Nurturing social-emotional development of gifted children', in K.A. Heller, F.J. Monks and A.H. Passow (eds.) *International Handbook for Research on Giftedness and Talent*, Oxford: Pergamon Press.

Welsh, M.C. and Pennington, B.F. (1988) 'Assessing frontal lobe functioning in children: Views from developmental psychology', *Developmental Neuropsychology*, 4, 199–230.

Westby, C. (1999) 'Assessment of pragmatic competence in children with psychiatric disorders', in D. Rogers-Adkinson and P. Griffith (eds.) *Communication Disorders and Children with Psychiatric and Behavioural Disorders*, San Diego: Singular Publishing Group.

Whitehurst, G.J., Falco, F.L., Lonigan, C.J. *et al.* (1988) 'Accelerating language development through picture book reading', *Developmental Psychology*, 24: 552–559.

Whitmore, J.R. and Maker, C.J. (1985) *Intellectual Giftedness in Disabled Persons*, Rockville, MD: Aspen.

Wilkins, A. (2003) *Reading Through Colour*, Chichester: John Wiley & Sons, Ltd.

Woodward, J. and Reith, H. (1997) 'A historical review of technology research in special education', *Review of Educational Research*, 67(4): 503–536.

Woolley, J.D. (1995) 'The fictional mind: Young children's understanding of imagination, pretense, and dreams', *Developmental Review*, 15(2): 172–211.

Wolf, M. (1991) 'Naming speed and reading: The contribution of the cognitive neurosciences', *Reading Research Quarterly*, 26: 1231–1241.

Wolf, M. and Bowers, P.G. (1999) 'The double-deficit hypothesis for the developmental dyslexia', *Journal of Educational Psychology*, 91: 415–438.

Wolfendale, S. (ed.) (1997) *Meeting Special Needs in the Early Years*, Exeter: David Fulton.

Wolfendale, S. (2000) 'Special needs in early years: prospects for policy and practice', *Support for Learning*, 15(4): 147–151.

Wray, D. and Shilvock, K. (2003) *Cross-Curricular Literacy 11–14*, London: Letts Educational.

# Index